VERMONT
R I V E R

W. D. Wetherell

Illustrations by Gordon Allen

Lyons & Burford, Publishers

Some of the chapters in this book appeared previously, as follows: "The River in Winter," *Gray's Sporting Journal,* Spring 1984; "Quadrangles," under the title "A Topographic Journey," *Country Journal,* February 1984; "A Trout for Celeste," *Appalachia,* April 1984; "Take a Writer Fishing," *The American Fly Fisher,* August 1984; "October Nineteenth," *Vermont Life,* Autumn 1984.

PRINTED IN THE UNITED STATES OF AMERICA
10 9 8 7 6 5 4 3 2 1

Library of Congress Cataloging in Publication Data

Wetherell, W. D., 1948–
    Vermont river.

    "Nick Lyons books."
    1. Fly fishing—Vermont. I. Title.
SH456.W38 1984   799.1' 1' 09743   84–1144
ISBN 0-8329-0365-5

FOR CELESTE

Contents

OOO

Preface to the 1993 Edition

∞

You never forget your first one. Ten years ago, having by hard work and considerable luck created for myself a life in the country, I fell in love with a trout stream a short distance from my home. Right from the start, *Vermont River* was conceived as an unabashed love letter to that river—and love letters, of course, aren't noted for being sober or constrained. Indeed, what strikes me most, reading it back, is how above all this is a young man's book, though it was written by a person approaching middle age. The note of lyrical enjoyment—where else could it have come from but my joy in being free of the city at last, my sense that now, after many years of trying, I was at last not only *where* I wanted to be, but *who* I wanted to be as well.

There are enough clues scattered throughout the book that many readers have guessed the river's identity. If it remains simply "the river" here, it's because I would again insist on the representational quality the water has for me, how it stands for many rivers fished before—and since. And while most of my fishing is elsewhere now, in bigger, harder rivers, or, conversely, quieter places with my kids, the river remains my trout fishing standard of measure, and the first thing I do on any new stream is compare it, for better or worse, with the one described here.

It's ten years now since *Vermont River* first appeared. A lot can happen in that time, to rivers and men, but fate can sometimes be gentle, and if I were writing the book today, not much would have to be changed.

I suppose there would be an angrier tone in parts, not so much at wanton destruction . . . for the river has so far escaped this . . . but at the damage caused by the peculiarly depressing form of human ignorance that doesn't recognize and value beauty when it's literally right under our nose. Of all my hunches of ten years ago, one is of particular relevance: that too many trout streams just simply disappear, not with the spectacular kind of bang that gets the big conservation organizations up in arms, unites fishermen, but in the sadder whimper of obscurity and neglect.

But I don't want to end on this note. *Vermont River*, more than any of my books, has brought me new friends. A man who sends me flies every year to try out on the trout; a woman who said it got her started fishing; friends who don't fish at all, but enjoyed it just the same; readers who, first knowing me through the book, have since become my fly fishing partners and confidantes. That's the one important thing I know now I didn't know then—how beautiful it can be to share a river with someone who loves and appreciates it as much as you do yourself. It's for winning these friends that I value the book the most.

The line in *Vermont River* that remains my favorite? The dedication, which, ten years later, remains in full and glorious force.

—W.D. Wetherell
April 1993

Vermont River

∞

The perfect river does not exist.

It takes a second to write the phrase, twenty years to learn it. The lesson is drummed in every time a fisherman goes out. Plans are planned, hopes hoped, dreams dreamt, and subtly but surely the magic river of our desire begins to flow—a trickle at first, widening to embrace our fondest imaginings, deepening to hold our longed-for trout, eventually carving out a channel that can seem so real and attainable that it dooms all actual rivers to insignificance. No river can match the rivers of our imagination. We stock them with fourteen-inch trout that rise readily to the fly, grace them with abundant shade and gentle breezes, preserve them from harm. There are no dams in our imaginary rivers. No pollution, no highways, no debris. They run unsullied between immaculate banks, our own inviolable preserve.

The river in this book is not imaginary. Were it, I would make some of the pools deeper, put them further from the road, inhabit them with bigger browns and shyer brookies. As beautiful as they are, the trout rivers that flow into the Connecticut in Vermont are not wilderness streams, and the towns that border them have their poverty and trailers and junkyards like everywhere else. Yet the realization that the river is less than my ideal subtracts not one iota from my enjoyment. Perfect rivers being mythical, the fisherman must adjust as best he can, finding what pleasure there is in the reality of it, facing up to the river's blemishes, trying to right them when he can, not letting thoughts of sylvan streams just beyond the horizon torture him into false comparisons. "Here I will begin to mine," Thoreau said, knowing that truth was as attainable in the woods around Concord, Massachusetts, as it was in the cities of Europe or the mountains of Tibet. It is with this same determination that I have decided to write about what the river has come to mean to me.

Readers familiar with Vermont will have little trouble identifying my river. If I have left it nameless, it is not for protective secrecy but because to me it stands for the dozen New England rivers I have come to know in twenty years of sometimes hard, sometimes casual fly-fishing. Indeed, so similar are their qualities that my river could well be the epitome of them all, could actually be part of the same overlapping flow, making it seem as though I have been slowly fishing up the rest of them toward it all along. Vermont's Battenkill or New Haven, Grand Lake Stream in Maine, Connecticut's Housatonic, the Quashnet of Cape Cod . . . this book might have been written about any one of them, and there is not a memory or observation in these pages that didn't have its germination on one of their banks.

This book covers a year on the Vermont river I love. Mostly it deals with fishing, sometimes with the absurd, humorous aspects of the sport. Little advice will be found here. I am a writer first, not a fisherman, and the insights I am after have little to do with catching more trout.

Fly-fishing is a discipline that in sensitive hands can account for a special perspective, putting its practitioners by its very nature into a closer, more harmonious association with the river they fish. When the fly fisherman goes empty-handed to the river, merely to sit and watch, he notices half the incidents and events he would notice if he brought a rod, the concentration fly-fishing demands being the price of admission to the intimacy he's after. Novelists are aware of the mysterious process by which the hidden truth of a situation or character often comes unbidden at the typewriter, revealed only in the act of being written down. So too with fly-fishing: the truth of a river comes in fishing it. Merge the fisher and the writer, merge the river and the word.

The perfect river does not exist. My Vermont river does. Here then, its exploration.

1

The River in Winter

∞

Having grown to love the river in the course of a season's fishing, I decided to revisit it in winter to see how it fared as snow and ice. It was a quick, unpremeditated decision; I went with a curious and fraternal feeling, as if to a seldom-seen friend, expecting it to be different but essentially unchanged. The river isn't long—seventeen miles if you iron out every bend, forty if you include the trout water on its two main branches. As closely as possible I would follow the length of it from its mouth at the Connecticut to its source back up in the mountains in the short daylight hours of one February day.

I left the house before dawn, in time to be caught in a snow squall that kept my speed down around twenty. There weren't any other cars out yet, and the only sign of life visible through the slanting flakes were the soft yellow lights from barns. In summer, I make the drive in half an hour, driving faster than I should, my mind caught between the writing I've just left and the fishing ahead of me, my nerves a turmoil of both. That morning, though, I was between novels, between trout seasons, and there were no ungrasped metaphors or streamside tactics to torment me. The quiet solitude of the road, the soft drape of flakes matched perfectly my own contentment.

The diner comes conveniently halfway on the trip. It's a welcome sight that time of morning, its warmth and light too tempting to pass up. A magazine had just given it an award for the best cup of coffee in

1

the state, and this is what I ordered—a big, thick mug with cream. It was crowded: telephone repairmen, construction workers, lumbermen, drivers. Their low voices and laughs went well with the clatter of plates. Someone had put a quarter in the jukebox to play a song three times, and as I nursed my coffee, Juice Newton's voice repeated the same lilting phrase over and over: "Blame it on the queen of hearts."

Back outside, the snow had stopped. The highway here is pinched in by cliffs, and whatever dawn there was in the sky stayed hidden until I broke clear of them south of town. I crossed the river on the Main Street bridge, parked in a lot by the post office and started down a snowy bank intending to walk the short distance to the river's mouth.

It was officially sunrise now, but directly east are the White Mountains and it's always a few extra minutes before the sun clears the peaks. Looking back toward town in the gray light, I could see the glacier-carved terraces down which the river falls in three abrupt steps: the steep upper terrace leading back from the dam into the valley; the flat, crowded plain of the town itself; the matching flood plain below town over which the river curves to a gentle intersection with the Connecticut.

Part of the lower terrace has been made into a golf course—the flag pins waved in the drifts like the lonely pennants of a polar expedition. A band of oaks marked the river bed, and without them it would have been difficult to determine where the stubble-dotted white of the cornfield on the opposite shore became the unblemished white of the river. It's at its widest here, lazy and almost delta-like. I climbed down the snow-matted sedge on the bank, intending to use the river as my path, but the ice cracked under me, and after a few tentative yards I retreated back to the trees. At least I could *see* where the river entered the Connecticut, and I decided that I was close enough to say I was there.

The sun was up now, and with it came various sounds, making it seem as if all the scrapings and bangings, whispers and skids that comprise a town's morning had been waiting for the sun's energy to give them voice. A dog barked. A horn beeped. The river, muted by ice as it spilled over the dam, made a sound like wind through foliated trees. Of all these sounds, though, the one I fastened onto was both the steadiest and most subtle: the sibilant, folding lap of water racing between banks.

Sure enough, there it was behind me, missed in my hurry to get to the mouth: an open stretch of river extending for a hundred yards or more below the dam. Walking toward it, my adrenalin started pumping; ludicrously, I found myself wishing I had brought my fly rod. I stared at the running water trying to memorize its color and texture, then hurried back up the cliff to town, anxious now to reach the part of the river I knew best.

I took the long way around to my car, walking beneath the tarnished Christmas decorations that—two months after Christmas— still overhung Main Street. The town was coming to life. By the falls, the carpenters restoring the 1847 mill sorted out their tools. A man with a Santa Claus belly unlocked the laundromat across the street, paused to spit toward the river. An old woman wheeled a shopping cart up the steep sidewalk. Above them by the library, the statue of a Spanish-American War admiral, town born, squinted warily toward the east with poised binoculars, as if expecting Cervera's Spanish fleet to come steaming up the Connecticut in battle formation. Just as the river is the epitome of Vermont rivers, the town could be the epitome of Vermont towns: battered, living half in the past, but with a sense of itself more fashionable places will never know. Close your eyes, then open them again. The plume of spray gushing over the dam, the slender stalactites on its fringe, the musty Victorian commercial buildings cheek by jowl with the simpler Colonial homes, the smell of wood smoke, the view of the mountains, the forty-eight stubborn stars on the flag before the American Legion's 150-year-old-hall—you could be nowhere else.

The alternate road out of town follows the river toward the mountains. There are a sawmill, a few old houses, then—just before the comparatively rich soil of the valley gives out—a last red farm, its back turned resolutely on the forest behind it. Beyond this is trout water, fifteen rushing yards from bank to bank, and as I drove along it one part of me tried to take in what I was actually seeing, while the other part raced back toward the summer and was caught up with swirling afternoon light and quick strikes and the feel of a trout trembling exhausted in my hand.

This is how it should be in winter. A river is a better metaphor than most, and half-frozen it becomes a blend of anticipation and recollection, flowing one moment toward the future, one moment toward the past. Proust, were he a trout fisher, might have summoned his remembrances in the Loire or some other French stream, finding its ripples and currents as evocative as the richest, most memory-laden of wines.

There is a cutoff by the first deep pool, and this is where I pulled over and got out. The previous May I had come here for the first time. Wading against the steep current to a smaller pool between an island and a cliff, I had caught a trout on my first cast—to a fisherman, never readier for miracles than on his initial try in new water, the most propitious of omens. The trout (admittedly, a small rainbow) went skipping across the surface as if to beach himself on the island, then changed his mind and headed straight for me as if to surrender. I am heretical in many angling habits, but none so much as in the landing of fish. By the time I've hooked a trout and controlled its first run, I begin to see things from its point of view, and after a few more minutes, have no particular desire to land it—in fact, I'm rooting for it to break off. (Once on Long Island's Connetquot, I fought a ten-pound brown—a world-class fish—for forty-five minutes, and was positively *relieved* when, in trying to beach him, he slithered out of my arms.) This first rainbow, though, came to me like a puppy on a leash, and when I twisted the Muddler out of his lip, he hovered by my leg in the current as if reluctant to leave.

I walked down to the river through the snow, half-expecting to see that same trout swim up to me, wagging its dorsal fin in recognition. But there was little chance of that. The pool where I caught him was now a jumbled mass of ice, resembling pictures I've seen of the Khumbu icefall on Everest. The entire channel on the far side of the island was frozen, and the only open water was the stronger current at my feet. The weather had turned dry after a stormy spell earlier in the month, and the river level had dropped dramatically, stranding the old ice. It was piled on the bank to a height of four or five feet, extending three or more yards back from the river, laying in glacier-like slabs and blocks, some square as tables, others all sharp edges and points. The plates nearest the river had debris embedded in their exposed edges: fallen leaves, sticks, even small logs. I stepped on one of the largest ice floes, and it immediately broke away downriver, carrying me with it like Little Eva, and I had to do some fancy boulder-hopping to get back to shore. Chastened, I climbed inland a few yards and paralleled the river upstream through the safer snow.

The banks get steeper here. Before long I was thirty feet above the river. Some of the trees had been marked with orange paint for cutting, but the blazes were old ones; the road crews had overlooked them, and I used their branches to brace myself from sliding down. At a point where the road curves right and climbs uphill is the most productive pool on the river: the Aquarium, a deep, lazy flow at the foot of a sharp rapid. In an afternoon's fishing I would catch upward of fifteen trout there without changing positions. Now, though I could peer right down into it, I saw no fish. The weak sunlight washed everything into an impenetrable gray.

Further upstream the banks level off, and I was able to cross an ice bridge over a small tributary and make my way to the water. The snow that covered the ice there had a puffy look to it, like the crust on a freshly baked pie. The river itself was half slush, half ice depending on where the sun hit it—ice dissolved into slush where it was brightest; slush crystallized into ice in the shade. In the middle, where the current was strongest, the water flowed against the ice with the gentle slapping sound of a sailboat on a downwind reach.

There was little color in that landscape, and when my eye happened to catch something reddish-orange on the opposite shore, the effect was that of a match flaring suddenly in the dark. Determined to get closer, I picked out a spot where the river was widest and thinnest and started to cross, risking hypothermia with every step. The dash of color turned out to be a Mickey Finn streamer embedded neatly in the branch of a willow, its monofilament tag blowing in the breeze. It had to be mine—I fished the Aquarium all season without seeing another fly-fisherman—and getting down on my hands and knees to penetrate the tangle, I quickly found three more flies, all broken off within a foot of each other: a bushy Bivisible, a tattered Light Hendrickson, a rusty

Muddler. In order to fish the far end of the pool, it's necessary to wade chest deep, putting even a high back cast perilously close to the branches. At a dollar or more a fly, it's an expensive place to fish. I searched through the trees some more without success, then stuck the four salvaged flies in the wool of my ski hat.

Back to the car, through a wind sharp enough to bring tears to my eyes. I poured a mugful of hot tea from the thermos and sipped it as I drove upriver. Above the Aquarium, the river flattens out for three miles, a broad, rocky stretch reminiscent of the Housatonic Meadows. The gentler grade had given the ice more leisure to do its work, and it was frozen solidly from bank to bank. Anticipation was becoming more urgent as I moved upriver; I resolved to come back to the flats during June when the insect hatches were at their peak—in June and at night, when the browns would be on the rise.

The South Branch meanders in here, but the dirt road that parallels it was too icy to chance on my bald, impoverished-novelist's tires, so I continued along the main river. My favorite stretch lay ahead, a series of pine-shaded riffles and pools that compose a landscape out of any fisherman's dreams. The moment I pulled over, I realized the beauty was still there—if anything, the winter had only enhanced it. The sun had come out. The water streamed past snow-covered ice islands, long, flat and narrow, the mirror image of the smooth granite ledges on the bottom, making it seem as though the river had been turned over and dusted white. As I made my way along the banks, I subconciously began to fish—dropping a fly in the eddy at the ice's prow, letting it drift down the edge of the miniature berg to the pool below.

It was on this stretch in early October that I met Doctor McKenzie. I had been fishing hard all day with little to show for it except weather and foliage so perfectly autumnal that they seemed like a cliché. On the rocks near shore were some of those furry, orange-and-black caterpillars that Vermonters like to claim portend a heavy winter. Tying on an orange Wooly Worm to imitate them, I was rewarded with a solid strike in the pool below the falls—one of my rare browns. I was releasing him when I heard a car door slam back up on the road. Turning, I saw a leprechaun slide feet-first down the bank.

I say leprechaun in all the gentle, sparkling sense of the word.

Doctor McKenzie—for so he introduced himself—was eighty-three years old and about five feet high, a retired surgeon who had traveled all the way from British Columbia to photograph the beauty of New England in the fall. He had a camera and tripod. He asked me to stay in place until he could cross the river and set up his gear.

Now I must admit that I made a pretty picture that day. When fishing, I usually wear an old chamois shirt and battered jeans, stuffing my fly boxes into whatever pockets happen to be available. That day, though, I was dressed as immaculately as an Orvis model: close-fitting waders, fishing vest, swordfisherman's hat, the works. Add to that a backdrop of forest at its most vivid red and shimmering gold and you have a calendar shot just begging to be taken.

"I've been looking all day for this," Doctor McKenzie said, excited as a boy. "Beautiful! It's absolutely beautiful!"

I was flattered, of course, but worried, too. I simply didn't see how a man so old and frail-looking could cross through that current without being swept away. I picked out the spot where I would plunge in to rescue him before he went flying over the falls, but it wasn't necessary—he waded through the rapids as daintily and gracefully as a heron, setting his tripod up on the one dry rock left above the foam.

He was there forty minutes and more, snapping away as I cast, muttering to himself in delight, signalling me to move here and there as the light dictated. When he finished, I followed him back to the car and we talked. He must have assumed I was playing hooky, because he assured me several times that my face wouldn't be recognizable in the picture, that he only wanted me to complete his setting. When he left, he handed me his card. Later that night over dinner, I told the story to Celeste and dropped the card on the table. Celeste, retrieving it, wrote the good doctor without telling me, and on Christmas morning I opened a package to find the picture beautifully framed: me, the river and the trees, as perfect a souvenir as that autumn day deserved.

Some of those same trees were fallen over now, their uppermost branches splayed across the water as if, tiring of winter, they had flung themselves there from desperation. I am tree lover enough to mourn their falling, but fisherman enough to wonder if the new eddies and currents formed around their trunks will create holding places for trout

come spring. Before, I had always thought of the winter as a quiet time
when the river slept, but in the course of that day I found that exactly
the opposite is true. The pressure from the built-up ice, the constant
change back and forth from liquid to solid to liquid, the runoff from
the snow—it's in winter that the river is being shaped, its weaknesses
tested. The life *in* the water may be relatively dormant, but the life *of*
the water is never more active.

The forest pools give way to a miniature canyon here—a dark,
shadowy place where I am never comfortable. At the head of it, I
walked back on the ice, lured by a fresh pattern of tracks. Deer tracks
first, their pattern disappearing into the half-frozen slush in midstream.
Fox tracks paralleled them—neat rows that as they neared the edge
suddenly became skid marks. I laughed, thinking of the fox slamming
on the brakes to avoid a dunking. There were other, smaller tracks,
too, patterns that went every which way, as if left by creatures who
had met there to dance a complicated quadrille. All the tracks were
centered in an area no bigger than a pool table, giving the effect of an
African waterhole. I wondered why they preferred this spot and no
other.

There was a subterranean gurgle beneath my feet. I knelt, brushed
away the snow from the ice. Through it, I could see milky bubbles
running back and forth like disoriented atoms, trying either to flee the
ice altogether and join the current or find a roughness to which they
could adhere. One after the other found a small edge; a few minutes
more and they were all pressed together, waving back and forth with
the lambent quality of flame.

I had been concentrating so much on the river that I'd lost track of
the weather. The promise that was in the sun had been blotted out by
clouds, and as I headed back to the car it began to snow. I'd have to
hurry to reach the headwaters; reluctantly, I passed up the fork in the
road that leads along the beautiful North Branch, and continued on the
main stream, past what surely must be the smallest ski area in the state
of Vermont, then a cemetery, its stark granite markers silhouetted
against the snow like miniature Stonehenges, then a small farm. Most
Vermont river valleys narrow and close in upon themselves as you
approach the headwaters, but here the landscape opens and spreads

apart, admitting wider vistas of light and sky. The knobby hills and open meadows reminded me of the highlands of Scotland, the lonely road that travels from Inverness to Ullapool.

Signs of life were infrequent. Snowmobile tracks across a deserted field. A tireless car drifted in snow. Billboards so faded and illegible that they've escaped Vermont's prohibition: Blue Seed Fee, Nana's Craft Shop, Maple Syrup 500 Feet. At a point where the river narrows, I saw the first people out enjoying it besides me: a group of school children using their recess to ice-skate on the overflow.

It was past three now, and I remembered I was hungry the same time as the general store appeared up ahead on the right. I know too many loquacious Vermonters to accept the laconic stereotype, but the clerk behind the counter made me think twice.

"Cold out," I said, blowing on my hands.

On cautious eyebrow half-raised. Yes.

"Have any coffee?"

The lips, already pencil thin, thinner. No.

"This snow supposed to last?"

He threw discretion to the wind and ventured to half-raise his eyebrow and tighten his lips at the same time, as if to say any damned fool knew that snowstorms in that part of the state *always* lasted.

He was right about that. When I went back outside with my Twinkies, snow covered the road and I had to drive it at a crawl, my wipers in a losing battle with the ice.

The river—brook trout water now—was further from the road here, only visible by the row of bare trees lining its bank. Another mile and it was obvious that this was as far as I was going today. As I pulled over to turn around, the snow slackened for a minute, letting the sun shine through the clouds. Ahead of me, I saw the twin mountains in the shadow of which the river has its source. The view was gone within seconds. The snow fell back into place with doubled intensity, giving the effect of a curtain that had been teasingly raised, then immediately dropped.

I needed to get to the river once more before going home. Taking a chance that the plows wouldn't be by for a while, I left my car on the side of the road and started through a field toward the trees. It was a part of the river I don't know well, and the seesaw I'd been riding between recollection and anticipation tipped decisively toward the future. The river is narrow here, dwindling toward its first springs and beaver ponds. Watching it, I promised myself I'd come back after black fly season and follow its windings to its source. It felt good to make a promise; it joined with the vow I'd made to teach Celeste to fly-fish, the vow to pick some lazy summer day to float the length of the river in inner tubes, the vow to learn how to fish a nymph once and for all, my vow to catch more and bigger browns.

The ice extended bank to bank, and the only break in the monotony was a small hole a few yards downstream. In the disorienting gray, the blinding snow, it assumed a significance out of all proportion to its size, looming in my imagination like one of those black holes in space that, collapsing, take with it all matter in its reach, becoming pure essence. The hole below me was the essence of my Vermont river, and as I turned regretfully to go, something bright and silver rose toward the middle, and faster than I can write it down was gone.

A trick of ice? A surge of water? A trout?

Spring will tell.

2

Quadrangles

∞

E very March, I go temporarily nuts over maps. Not just any maps. Oil company maps, *National Geographic* maps, maps tucked in guidebooks, street maps, atlases and globes all leave me cold. Maps on place mats, maps on matchbooks, maps on ashtrays or cribbage boards I positively despise. No, the focus of my addiction is much more limited, but infinitely more detailed: the beautiful green and brown topographic maps of the United States Geological Survey.

The local hardware store stocks them, in a fine metal case where the sheets lie immaculate without folds. The complex but rewarding Camels Hump quadrangle of 1948; the state-straddling Mt. Cube of 1931; the modern, somewhat mundane East Corinth of 1973; the vintage, all but legendary East Barre of 1957, companion of some of my happiest map-browsing hours . . . Mr. Waite's chest contains them all. On rainy afternoons I'm apt to spend a good hour or more going through them, tracing contour intervals up mountains I've hiked, following trout streams to their obscurest tributary, spreading the maps out on the wooden floor to match them to their neighbors, not stopping until a gentle inquiry from Mr. Waite makes me replace them sheepishly in their bins.

Occasionally, I even buy one; at three dollars a fix, they are among the cheaper addictions. I have four maps spread on the carpet below me as I write, their corners weighted down with fly reels. It is too warm and muddy to go skiing, too cold yet for fishing, and I am neither fly-

13

tier nor hobbiest. The maps fill a vacuum, use up time that hangs heavy in the long weeks before spring. But they are more than that, too, and my fascination with them is comprised of many elements—their beauty, their elaborate detail, the mysteries they offer, the discoveries they reveal.

Beauty first. Even as mere objects, topographic maps are attractive things, and even less-inspired efforts like the East Corinth quadrangle are of gallery quality. They even *feel* nice; the crisp, no-nonsense paper reeks of trustworthiness and good sense. In unrolling it, the edges will tug gratifyingly on your fingers, as if the paper has a life and will of its own.

Hung on a wall and seen from a distance, topographic maps resemble late Van Goghs, with swirls and coils, eleborate circles and extravagant loops. The contour lines in their convoluted twistings are as suggestive as ink blots, forming here a butterfly or amoeba, there a breaker or cloud. Color is everywhere. Blue streams curve across brown contour lines over green forests. Red roads bisect black boundary markers by aquamarine ponds near terra cotta cities, and all is centered perfectly in broad, even margins of white.

But as beautiful as the colors are, I think the deepest beauty topographic maps offer is more cerebral: here spread before you is a small, comprehensible portion of the earth, its hills and valleys lovingly traced, its man-made additions duly marked, its unceasing hurry for one moment checked.

Within these lines and symbols there is much to explore. But a word of caution is in order. If there is one hazard in being addicted to topographic maps, it is in the danger of being overwhelmed by their detail, not seeing the mountains for the contour lines. After years of puzzling over them, I've begun to understand some of the basic details; i.e., that a 15–minute quadrangle covers a square that is fifteen minutes of longitude by fifteen minutes of latitude, and that a 7.5–minute quadrangle covers a quarter of that area with correspondingly greater detail (but with less sweep and breadth of view). I also understand about contour intervals; if the contour interval is twenty feet, then any point on a contour line is twenty feet above or below any point on the neighboring contour line. Scale is just as easy; if it's 1:62500, then any unit such as an inch or centimeter on the map equals 62,500 of the same units on the ground. The magnetic declination diagram in the margin shows how far magnetic north differs from true north—nothing tricky there. I know about bench marks, too, having tripped over one while fishing once, and given a good ruler, I can handle mileage scales tolerably well.

Some things, however, are mysterious. Grid ticks, for instance. Are they yardage markers in football or a new species of insect pest? On the East Corinth quadrangle are several small patches that are comprised of green polka dots. What could they possibly mean? Could there still be corners of Vermont that are terra incognita, polka dots being the government's way of saying they have no idea what's there?

After wondering about these and other equally arcane symbols, I finally sent to the U.S. Geological Survey in Virginia for a folder describing topographic maps in detail. Grid ticks turn out to be "a network of uniformly spaced parallel lines intersecting at right angles," useful for engineers and their ilk. Green polka dots turn out to represent an orchard—in Vermont, an apple orchard more than likely. Three wavy lines in a river means rapids or falls. A straight line with crewcut hair growing out of it means a wooded marsh.

Some of the more interesting symbols aren't likely to be found on Vermont quadrangles. Green polka dots that are more tightly bunched than those for an orchard depict vineyards. A sinking ship represents an exposed wreck. A pretty green floral design means a mangrove swamp. A box with little curls in it means a lava field; a little triangle, oil wells. My favorite is a small black circle with a crescent on the top. The meaning? "A mosque or Sheikh's tomb."

There is a lesson in all this, and it is a simple one. If topographic maps are the most precise of precision instruments, then they are also the most suggestive, and an active imagination can find hours of pleasure in poring over them in wonder.

Take the quadrangle unfolded before me now, the one that maps the upper reaches of my favorite trout river. It's probably as close as you can come to a typical 15–minute swatch of Vermont, including as it does two or three mountains, a score of hills, a whole network of unimproved dirt roads, idiosyncratic boundaries, several small hill towns, two or three "notches," at least one "hollow," and enough cemeteries hidden away in the forest to hint at how many human lives ran out there in the century before. The place names are a joy to say aloud: Michigan Hill, Duplissey Hill, Lyme Emery Hill, Pike Hill, Hurricane Ridge, Mount Pleasant; Riders Corner, Riddle Pond, Foster Notch, Hart Hollow, Goose Green . . . each one suggesting a story, each one a monument to a time when every feature of the Vermont terrain was familiar enough to some caring soul to be called by name.

A legend on the bottom of the map says that it was "compiled in part from aerial photographs taken in 1938," and as I look at it, I picture a yellow biplane circling the ridges, a camera mounted on its wing, the plane soaring on the updrafts on a Vermont summer day. For it is an aerial, bird's-eye view that topographic maps provide—run your eyes quickly from top to bottom and the effect is as dizzying as flight. And nothing short of flight gives you such a quick appreciation of terrain. The two symmetrical mountains between which the river has its source, the ones that always look to me like twins? Sure enough, there they are on the map, both topping out at exactly 3166 feet, proof to the eye. That steep ridge above the pool in the river where I caught that big rainbow trout last June, the ridge beyond which I could never see? There it is, the contour lines pressed together like isobars, and beyond it is a plateau in the middle of which is a swamp. That tiny stream that comes into the main river over a miniature falls? I trace it back into the hills, find its source in a small pond a mile and a half above the river, vow to fish up to it come May.

There are houses back in the hills, tiny black squares that form the human dimension in the crosshatches and grids. Beside some of them are the white squares that represent barns; when they are connected barns, the white and black squares are joined. I imagine my way up to the most remote of them, my finger running west out of the small hill town that straddles the river (the homes, the church, the school are all depicted, the last with a little flag), tracing my way past the small cemetery, passing one or two lonely houses strung along the high open meadows beyond town, then entering the woods as the road turns to dirt. I can picture the ruts in that road, picture the humpbacked middle, the way that steep ridge pinches it in toward the stream. The house, by my ruler, is a mile further—not a house really, but a cabin, sharing a small clearing with a fallen-down barn, nest to owls. That nameless hill behind the house (elevation 2418) must catch a lot of the sun—night comes early in the late summer and fall. Looks like that swamp at its base must breed clouds of mosquitoes. Then, too, the nearest house is three miles—lonely place for a wife and kids. No wonder the barn is fallen down and abandoned. No wonder the town never votes to improve the road. No wonder it's lost now, lost except for this lonely black square on a forty-year-old map.

These journeys to polka dotted fields and abandoned hill farms I may never actually make, but there are other trips that I will start upon and topographic maps will be an inestimable aid when I do. This is the year I've promised myself that I'll follow my favorite river to its source, much the way Speke and Burton traced the Nile. Fishing the headwaters, it's hard to know which of numerous branches that form the main stream *is* the main stream. On the map, all is clear. The ultimate winding of the river departs from the highway opposite a small cemetery (elevation 1827), parallels a dirt road that shortly ends (good place to leave the car), and climbs through fairly gentle terrain for the first two miles, giving me time—once I start hiking—to limber up my legs. The contour lines gradually start closing up into arrowhead-shaped wedges—there may be falls here, forcing me to detour further from the bank in order to make any progress. After about half a mile, the contour lines flatten out, the mountains open up a bit, and with most of the climb behind me, it will be a fine spot to eat my lunch. Another hour should do it. The stream will become smaller and smaller, smaller than my stride, and I will cross it many times before I come to the spring in the ground that must be the river's highest source, smack on the crosshatched boundary lines of two Vermont counties.

Staring at the map, I can imagine the sound of that stream, feel the ache in my calfs as I climb, smell the breeze as it comes down off the mountains. But it is April now, the temperature climbs tentatively toward fifty, and as suddenly as my map-scanning passion came on, it is gone. Vicarious trips no longer suffice, blue lines make poor substitutes for streams, and stuffing the topographic maps in an old bookcase, I grab my fly rod and rush outside.

3

April Fourteenth

∞

The water, like the sky, had a scoured look to it. The dead reeds that lined the banks lay perfectly flat, as though a wire brush had been run through them a hundred times preparatory to spring—ninety-eight, ninety-nine, one hundred, smoothing them into a part, their tips all trending in the same direction. Above them, the sagging branches of uprooted trees touched the water, and where they touched the water their bark was burnished gold. Out in the current—the current which for its hard green brilliance might have been the coruscating agent itself—the rocks were as polished as gems. There was nothing extraneous in the landscape. It was stripped down to its elements—water and sky—the debris of winter washed away in one great torrent of brightness.

I went into it at the long stretch above the pine canyon, the part of the river I love most. The state of Vermont allowed me to fish beginning at 12:01 A.M. on Saturday, April 9, but I had chosen to start the trout season at my own convenience—at 8:01 A.M. on Thursday, April 14. Even later than that, as it turned out. For the season began this year, not when I got up in the morning, the adrenalin racing me through breakfast; not when I loaded my rods in the car and drove the thirty minutes of highway; not even when I first stepped into the current and began to cast. No, the season began at 8:05 or thereabouts, the moment when after picking my way gingerly around several huge

19

and dangerous ledges, I found myself twenty yards out in midstream with the full weight of the river on my thighs.

Of all the sensations associated with fly-fishing, this is the one linked most closely to spring. For if spring is energy—the light that lures crocuses from the soil, the warmth that birds track north—then this is energy made manifest, the pushing, rushing current breaking against your legs as you cast. Implicit in it are the fifteen miles of river upstream, all the tributaries to the river, all the tributaries to the tributaries, the trickles, runs, pools, drips and springs that comprise a watershed—all this is at your back, pressing your waders until the fabric clutches at your legs, pushing your feet out from their hard-won stance, supporting you when you lean against it, shivering you, even through lined pants and long underwear, with its chill. For all the current knows, you are part of the river itself, to be sprung against and pried at like any other rock or branch that gets in its way.

Current is the continuous note of a fly fisherman's day. All the casting, all the probing for trout, the tactics, are merely embellishments to that throb. And like any deeply felt sensation, it carries with it its own echo, so that even now, writing four days after I fished, I can feel the power of the river on my legs, a vague and very satisfactory hum.

The feel of it all—the sense of once again uniting muscles and nerves in harmonious, graceful ways—is one element of an April start. The other is more cerebral, depending as it does on the thread of memory that links the fisherman standing in the river to the boy who *dreamed* of standing in the river. Part of you is that boy, and the sensitivity to realize this is never sharper than on opening day when the dream is renewed with the most ceremony and deliberation.

I caught this thread several times that morning. The first was when I stopped in town to buy some flies. They lay in trays on the counter, bushy Marabou Streamers, slim Gray Ghosts, nymphs as hard and spare as stones. I picked through them with the same sense of anticipation I felt as a boy of fourteen buying lures to throw at bass on the Connecticut lake where I grew up.

It only lasted a few minutes. By the time I paid for them and went back outside to the car, my mind was back in the present, worrying how high the river would be. But the same thing happened again when I put together my fly rod at the river's edge; my hands shook just as they shook when I walked down to Candlewood Lake on opening day twenty years before. I went with the feeling this time, deliberately prolonged the link, until by the time I waded out to the middle of the river and began to cast, I was in some sense standing aside from myself, looking at this tall fisherman waist-deep in a Vermont river with the eyes of the boy who wished for nothing so much as to be one day standing in a Vermont river casting for trout.

The fulfillment of a childhood dream is fishing's deepest reward. I think of an eighty-year-old I met one fall on the Battenkill (an eighty-year-old, by the way, with three fat trout in his creel)—how he talked constantly of next season's opening day, even though the season wasn't yet ended. "If I'm still around, that is," he added cautiously when he mentioned his plans. Opening day, youth, one more chance—these were all clearly linked in his phrase, and I felt tender toward him, and marveled that childhood's excitement and need could persist so long.

Thus, April 14.

"Here I am," I thought as I stood there casting. "Here I *am!*"

The fourteen-year-old in me would have had me catch a trout—a big four-pounder, bright with spring—but the part of me that's thirty-four knew better, and I worked through the reach without really expecting to find any fish. The water was clear enough, but too high, fast and cold; the trout were still in a state of suspended animation, hungover from winter, in no mood to chase my fly. On the theory that cold water deserves a cold lure, I was fishing a Polar Bear Muddler, but on my third cast I snapped it off on a branch, and the rest of my flies seemed too summery to have much of a chance. I drifted a bucktail through the last pool, then climbed up onto the bank to warm myself in the sun.

There were some homemade doughnuts in my vest, compliments of Celeste. I ate them while I watched the river. On the opposite bank a flock of goldfinch assembled in a great congregation, darting from tree to tree in their swerving loops, chattering excitedly away. They're a common enough bird in Vermont, but I never seem to see them, and I welcomed the chance. I was wondering where these particular ones had

spent the winter when I noticed something out of the corner of my eye
in the river—a log, I thought at first. But when I turned my head to
look, it wasn't a log that I saw shooting past, but a kayak—a kayak
and a life jacket and a helmet. By the time I realized there was a man in
the center of all this, it was gone.

Three more came after that, spaced at intervals of about a minute.
Judging by the way they threaded the rapids, they were all experts;
there was an abrupt ledge above the canyon, but they steered right for
it, as if this were exactly the sort of challenge they were seeking.
Paddles windmilled back and forth as they fought to keep the kayaks
from swinging broadside to the current . . . a moment of suspense as
their bows shot over the ledge . . . then they were gone down the
canyon, trailing behind them the sound of their triumphant laughs.

Motion, color, dash. The kayaks made me feel sluggish and landbound, and I decided it was time to get back into the river. Not the
main river. If I was going to catch a trout that day, it would have to be
on one of the tributaries—the river itself was simply too high. I had
talked to a man down in Woodstock earlier in the week who had
caught his limit on one of the small feeders to the White. Nymphs, he
said. Weighted and brown.

I drove the three miles to the junction pool, crossed the river on the
new bridge and started up the road that runs back along the South
Branch. About a mile up, I pulled over and parked. I could hear the
stream before I could see it; the bank is overgrown here, and I had to
pick my way along it before I found an easy way down to the water.

The South Branch is much less pastoral than the main river, steeper
and more mountain-like. Even so, I was counting on less water—
during spring runoff, the higher tributaries usually clear first. What I
hadn't counted on, though, was that the valley had retained more of
winter, and there was still ice along both banks of the stream.

It was too late to back out. I crossed one of the ice slabs, and made it
to a rock below a likely looking pool. Casting quickly, I laid a Hare's-
Ear nymph on the spot where the current fanned apart, and let it
bounce down the middle of the pool toward my stance.

No response. I cast again, this time shading it a bit more to the left.
No response. The right side now, a slower drift. No response. I

abruptly switched directions, cast for distance, let the nymph swing across the current in pocket water above a downed tree. No response. I let the nymph drift below me, let it hang there like a worm.

I spent an hour or more fishing all the water within reach. Only once did the nymph stop its drift, but when I tightened, it was on a submerged branch, not a fish, and I broke off the fly. Since fishing was hopeless, I decided to hike upstream, prospecting for likely pools I could fish later in the month. But even this modest intention came to naught. Above this stretch the ice on the banks became thicker, the blowdowns more frequent, and by the time I gave up climbing and headed back to the car, I was sweating from effort.

I took the rod apart and was pulling off my waders when a pickup drove past, going far too fast for that narrow road. A hundred yards above me, it squealed to a stop, went into reverse, went fishtailing across the road and stopped six inches from my knees.

A man my own age got out, grinning from ear to ear.

"How's the fishing?"

I told him. As he listened, he kept nodding up and down, as if he were taking great delight in what I was saying. He had the lean, ascetic look of a marathon runner, but rather than jogging clothes, he wore battered work pants and a thin cotton shirt.

"You don't see many fly fishermen on this river," he said, once I finished.

I shrugged.

"I'm a fly fisherman," he said, with the slightly defensive air of someone who doesn't expect you to believe him.

And so we talked. He was out of work—the lumber industry, the housing slump—and was trying to cheer himself up by thinking about all the time it would give him to fish; "for dinner," he said, laughing. He was new to fly fishing, and I answered his questions as best I could. Yes, nymphs were probably best this time of year. No, I hadn't read Schwiebert's later article on stonefly imitations. Yes, it was a beautiful river. More than beautiful.

"Big browns down there," he said, tilting his head. "I'm going to fish at night this year. You ever fish much at night?"

He asked me what I did, and I told him. He listened to me complain about the book business for a while; I listened to him complain about logging, and that settled, we got back to the fishing again.

All the while we talked, I was bothered by something in my tone—a note of condescension and weary patience. Where did it come from? He was my age, after all, and there I was talking to him like that eighty-year-old on the Battenkill had once talked to me; it was all I could do not to call him "Sonny." I think it must have been the difference in ages between our dreams. Mine was established and mature; his was brand-new, resembling in its enthusiasm and rough edges my excitement at fourteen. No wonder I sounded so all-knowing and wise. The latest theories, the latest tackle—once upon a time I had been full of these myself.

"Hey, I've got to go," he said, for the fourth time in ten minutes. "See you on the river, right?"

"Look for me."

"Hope you sell more books."

"Thanks. Good luck with the job!"

I had been intending to quit for the day, but our talk left me feeling the dream again in all its original intensity, and I couldn't bear the thought of leaving. I ended up fishing the entire afternoon. There's no need to go into details. It was the stretch above the Aquarium, but for once there were no fish there, and I wouldn't have caught any if there were. I cast quickly and badly, changed flies much too often, slapped the line against branches, rocks and logs, twisted the leader into knots, waded into spots where I had no business being, and in short made every mistake a fly fisherman can possibly make. I was aghast at my behavior, of course, but deemed it necessary; after a winter cooped up indoors, my impatience was as high as the river, and like the current, must have its way.

Four hours in water a little above freezing works wonders. By the time I climbed out onto the banks in the soft light of dusk, I felt as scoured as the river itself, rid of all the staleness that was in me, washed of my impatience and ready—once more—to begin.

4

My Brilliant Career

∞∞

I t occurs to me that, at least on paper, I qualify as an expert on fishing. I could list my stories, which have appeared regularly in America's most prestigious fishing magazine, my time as an editor at another fishing publication, my career demonstrating fly rods for a famous tackle company in Vermont. To the nonfisherman, these accomplishments may seem as nothing, but to the fly fisher, it is roughly like saying that W. D. Wetherell is Ernest Hemingway, A. J. McClane and Charles Orvis all wrapped up into one.

This is troubling. Not because I have anything against these men, but because I distrust experts in general and fishing experts in particular. (This is not necessarily uncommon; I once met a man who had developed a bitter grudge against Jason Lucas, the old *Sports Afield* columnist, and vowed to drown him should he ever appear on the same lake.) Am I an expert myself then? One of those smug, insufferably knowledgeable bores who inhabit with pollsters and developers the lowest terrace in my personal modern-day inferno? Let us examine the evidence in more detail.

My short stories. They have indeed appeared in America's best fishing magazine (I'm entitled to call it that, having worked three years on the worst), but any fisherman trying to garner tips on landing more fish from them would probably be more likely to give up fishing altogether. One concerns a man who fishes for bass "in order to free

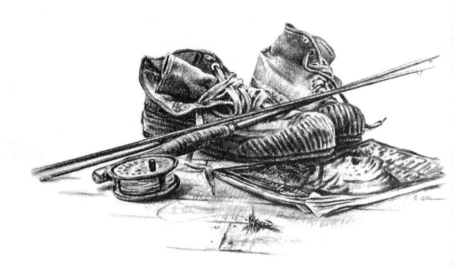

them from the mortal terror in which they swim'' and ends up succumbing one night to the same terror himself; one deals with a trout fisherman undergoing a mid-life crisis in a Manhattan bar; the third is about a man who goes to Maine to spread his dead brother's ashes on his favorite lake, and in doing so, absent-mindedly destroys his reputation at the fishing camp where he had gone for years. Whatever their value, these are not your usual me-and-Dad-fishing-for-old-Mossback-in-the-lake-no-one-knew-about-except-us-and-those-times-sob-are-now-gone-sob-forever stories. If I try to come up with an influence that was behind me as I wrote, it would be Kafka—Kafka as a fly fisherman in a long black coat, casting shyly in some Prague trickle, fishing for the absurd the way other men fish for trout.

This, of course, is a long way from A. J. McClane.

Harder to explain are the three years I spent as an editor at a New York magazine I'll call *Angling International.* In tackiness, *Angling International* was akin to some girlie magazines, the cheaper kind that look as if they're printed in Peru. Rather than bosoms and rear ends, *A.I.* featured shots of enormous, repulsive-looking bass, only we weren't allowed to call them bass, they were always "Hawgs!" with an exclamation point. Alliteration was very important in all our titles. *Hooked on Hawgs!, Horsing for Hawgs!* and *Hip Hip for Hawgs!* were typical. The circulation was claimed to be upwards of 100,000, but we at the magazine never had a hint that anyone actually read it, and it was the considered opinion of most of us that the publisher ran it as a tax dodge.

Like a lot of sad involvements, mine began with an ad in the *New York Times:* "Editor wanted who enjoys fishing." I had just graduated from college with a degree in philosophy, a passable roll cast and not much else. Wes, *Angling International*'s managing editor, was intelligent enough to accept the essential absurdity of the magazine, and in keeping with this understanding, was quirky enough to hire me, sight unseen, as assistant editor.

Wes himself did most of the work. It was my job to copy-edit the stories, proofread, write a column on new products and do some research. One of my first assignments involved an article on fishing in New Zealand. All the prices mentioned were in New Zealand dollars, and I was to convert them into their U.S. equivalents, the easier for our readers to plan their trip. Unfortunately, I used the wrong formula, dividing where I should have multiplied or vice versa, the result being that all the prices were converted into half the New Zealand amount when they should have been double, thereby making New Zealand appear the cheapest destination in the world. It was printed that way; I remember vividly the sad yet forgiving look on Wes's face when he learned of my error. Such mistakes were an inevitable accompaniment to his life, and even if they were someone else's fault, he naturally assumed they were his own.

We had another assistant editor, a blonde woman in her thirties who could neither fish, write nor spell. Joan was incapable of saying a sentence that didn't contain the word "hah" in it, and she would emit it with a honking, nasal intonation, like a goose. Depending on her mood, "hah" could be invitational, interrogative, denunciatory, decorative or prayerful—sometimes a mixture of all five. To this day, I'm not sure what she did at the magazine, but it must have been something.

We had some famous bylines in the magazine, fishing experts I had read and admired as a boy. As bad as it was, *A.I.* paid on time, and this attracted a lot of people who had to wait for their checks at the glossier publications. I was looking forward to working with these writers, and hoped that my involvement with them would lead to fishing invitations, free trips and gear.

Imagine my disappointment, then, to learn that some of these experts were for all intents and purposes illiterate, their careers having been established by rigged photographs and a great deal of cronyism of the old-boy-network variety. These weren't just bad writers, they couldn't write *at all;* much of my time was spent finding their subjects and predicates and linking them in some sort of reasonable order. It was a depressing task. It was 1974, the year of Watergate, and working on these ineffable manuscripts caused in me the same kind of disillusionment that other people were feeling toward politicians.

But like Wes, I gradually came to accept the essential ludicrousness of it all, and even began to enjoy it. Of all the *Angling International* absurdities, Wes himself was by far the most interesting. He looked like a fisherman—his eyes had a distant focus to them, as if they had spent hours studying rivers for the hatch; his body was slender and wiry, like so many good casters—and he was originally from Montana. But if the truth be known, Wes—editor of a large fishing magazine, writer of a superb column of angling advice read by thousands—did not fish.

What he did was sit in his office waving a fly rod around while he watched the elevated trains roll by. I rarely saw him do anything else. Occasionally, he would talk on the phone to one of our writers; occasionally, he would wander off to the art department and wave his fly rod around in there, but this was the limit of his small world. I would come back from weekend fishing trips full of stories, and he would listen to these with a look of haughty condescension on his face, as if to say that these amateurish junkets of mine were all very fine, but to a man who knew the Yellowstone . . . Well, someday he would explain.

It was a comfortable life, but then the day finally came when he was invited to go fishing out west by a famous fish and game organization. His face was white as he put down the phone. I think he realized that after five safe and lazy years, his bluff had been called.

There were too many past refusals on his part, too many last-minute cancellations for him to back out of it. He was gone three days. When I came to work the morning of the fourth day, he was at his usual place in the office, whisking the fly rod around with his left hand—his left hand because his right one was in a cast.

I never asked him about it and he never explained. From that day on, though, his column began to take on a bitter, mordant quality, and our receptionist had strict orders to screen all calls, making sure he was never asked to go fishing again.

This brings us to the third and seemingly most unshakeable pillar of my expertise—my time on the staff of a famous tackle company in Vermont. I may as well admit right at the start that I have occasionally taken advantage of this experience to assert myself in the subtle one-upmanship fly fishermen sometimes indulge in. For instance, I'll meet someone on the river who drops references to his trips to Labrador, his new Garrison rod, his good friend Lee Wulff.

"That's interesting," I'll say, stifling a yawn. "Reminds me of my time working at ———."

"Your time working at where?" he'll say in disbelief.

"My time working at ———."

"You worked at ———?" disbelief now turning to awe.

"Yeah, for a while. Is that a rise over there?"

Now saying you worked at ——— is roughly like saying you were in the Yankee outfield when Maris and Mantle were in their prime. And I did work there once, the summer I was nineteen.

It came about like this. I had bought enough flies through the mail to be on the company's mailing list; reading their newsletter one day, I saw an ad for a fly fisherman to work in their store for the May to October season. They had started a fishing school that year, and the regular salesmen would be teaching, creating the opening. I immediately sat down and wrote a long letter listing my fly-fishing credentials, making half of it up (most of my fly fishing at this time being strictly vicarious). About a week after mailing it, I received a call from the company's manager asking me to come to Vermont for an interview.

I took the bus from New York. During the interview, I kept stealing peeks at all the beautiful gear displayed on the walls: bamboo fly rods, canoes, waders... this soon could be mine! As nervous as I was, I managed to stay fairly calm under the manager's polite questions ("I see in your letter that you once caught an eight-pound rainbow on a #22 Adams. Tell me about that."). An hour later, when I walked back through the snow to the bus stop, I had the job.

The position began in May. I spent the intervening two months practicing my casting, studying every fishing book I could find, memorizing the diameter of 4X tippets, and in general trying to assimilate enough information to hide my lack of experience. I drove up to Vermont the day before I was scheduled to go to work. Needing to find a place to stay, I stopped first at the store. The manager introduced me to the other salesmen; like *Angling International,* the company was fond of alliteration, and everyone had a nickname that started with the same letter as his surname: Sip Simmers, Pete Peters, Rap Roberts and so on. Thus, I was introduced not by my first name (which, alliterative as it was, wasn't quite alliterative enough), but as "Weth Wetherell."

None of the salesmen seemed particularly interested in anyone called Weth Wetherell, and they quickly resumed their interrupted discussion. It was all about "The 'Kill"—the Battenkill River, which was right down the road. One of the men had caught ten brown trout in the space of an hour using a Yellow Muddler. Another man had caught eleven on a Strawberry Blonde. The third man had fished all day without catching anything. It was a pattern I saw repeated several times the following day; it was considered okay to brag about catching ten or more trout, okay to admit you had caught none, but somehow amateurish to admit anything between one and nine.

I found a temporary room at a house in town, and went to bed early, ready for the big day. I arrived an hour before the store opened: as before, no one seemed particularly interested in talking to me. When the manager arrived, he issued me the same kind of khaki fishing shirt

that everyone else was wearing, and explained what my duties would
be.

These were: (1) to help keep the stock in order; (2) to see that the
trout in the casting pond were fed each day; and (3) to help customers
when they came in, and especially people interested in fly rods.

This is what the company was all about—the expensive, exquisitely
crafted bamboo rods that lined one wall of the shop. Should a customer
want to try one out, we were to drop everything and go outside to the
casting pond with him, spending as much time as it took to make the
sale.

Fine. The manager patted me on the back and disappeared. Not
much happened for the first hour or so. I rearranged some fly boxes,
dusted off a display case, tried to strike up a conversation with Sip and
Rap. About eleven, a man came in dressed in a fishing vest. I asked if I
could help him, but he shook me off and went right to the book
display. Rap mentioned his name to me—he was a famous fishing
writer, one I had read as a boy. He had a pencil and pad with him. As it
turned out, this is how he did his research, cribbing from other
people's books, which he was too cheap to buy.

At noon, I went outside to feed the trout. They were expecting
someone—they crowded one side of the pond, and when I tossed the
fish chow to them, they exploded through the water like sharks. I
asked the manager if they had a poaching problem with the unfenced
pond being so close to the highway.

"You kidding?" he said, pointing to where the huge fish were
tearing apart the surface. "Kids in town are *scared* of them."

Feeding the trout proved to be the high point of the day. At
lunchtime, the salesmen sat on benches at one end of the pond
swapping stories, but I wasn't invited to join them, so I ate alone in
my car. I was beginning to feel a little sorry for myself—the job was
not turning out to be what I had imagined. Nothing happened during
the afternoon to improve things. Customers did start to trickle in, but
they were the worst kind of pompous, name-dropping snobs, and I
remember being puzzled at the humorless way they went about
selecting their equipment. It was a type I was to get to know better in

the years to come—the affluent, middle-aged American male, as joyless in his play as he was in his work—but at the time, they were new to me.

The worst of them was a tall man with a complexion the color of rust. He was going salmon fishing on the Miramachi, and wanted a "fly rod that wouldn't embarrass" him. I knew nothing about salmon fishing except that you needed a heavy rod, so I grabbed from the case the longest, thickest one I could find, mounted a reel on the bottom and led him outside to the pond.

Here was my chance. I would sell him this $300 fly rod, sell him a $100 reel and $20 line to go with it, and win the grudging respect of the other salesmen and my first commission besides.

"Nice rod," I said casually, threading the line through the guides. "One of our least embarrassing models."

I suggested that he try a few casts. They weren't very successful, partly because his cast technique was weak, but mostly because I had mounted it with a line that was far too light.

"Feels floppy," he said, frowning.

"I think it needs more forearm," I suggested.

Now the first rule in helping someone with a rod was *never in any way criticize his casting.* The man's face immediately reddened.

"I think I'd rather have someone else," he said.

I ignored him. "Here, I'll show you how."

I picked up the rod. Working out some line, I started false-casting toward the pond. Everything went fine until I had about fifty feet out, when between one moment and the next my carefully constructed dream fell apart. The line, alighting on the pond, was enough to suggest a fish-chow pellet to the still-hungry trout. One of them made a rise toward the tip of my leader. Instinctively striking back at him, the line whistled past my head toward the customer's. He ducked—I yanked on the line and sent it flailing back again toward the pond, only now it was completely out of control. I had one more chance, but I blew it; the line, undulating back again over my head, coiled itself around one of the benches near the parking lot. Before I could stop myself, I had started my forward cast again, and the moment the line tightened, the rod shattered apart in my hands.

For a moment, all was silence.

"Jesus," the man said.

Even at nineteen, I was writer enough to recognize an exit line when I heard one. Without saying a word, without telling anyone where I was going, I took off my fishing shirt, placed it carefully by the pond and voluntarily ended my brilliant career.

5

Symphony

∞

The 21st now, and seventeen of these days have seen rain, most of it torrential. Just when it became insupportable—just when the rain and dampness became permanent in our souls—we had a change. It began to snow.

Welcome to May in Vermont.

My bus-driving friend Ken Baker put it best. We were following a snowplow down toward Hanover, watching the unutterably depressing sight of flowers disappearing under a heavy outwash of white.

"Well," Ken said, lapsing into the thick Yankee accent he saves for his wriest profundities, "'twas a pretty good winter until spring got here."

Ayuh. But while I can come to terms with mudholes, leaky roofs and smothered tulips, I've had a harder time adjusting to what the rain has done to my river. It's unfishable, of course—so high and muddy and wide it reminds me of old black-and-white newsreels I've seen of the Mississippi in flood. And though my intellect registers that I have absolutely no business wading it, my instincts are programmed to May, and I gravitate toward its banks with all the free will of a withered daffodil caught up in its current.

I was a fisherman who—before drowning—badly needed a nudge. As it turned out, I got two, and both were gentler than I had any right to expect.

The first nudge was quite literal. I was casting in the rain above the longest of the river's bridges, the new steel one they put in last July. It's a thoughtful place to fish. On the left bank are the ruins of a century-old stone bridge the ice had long since washed out; on the right are the twisted beams of a more recent span, an arthritic victim of old age. I like the continuity there—fords are where the fates of rivers and man are longest entwined, and it's nice to be faced with reminders of their coexistence.

The sogginess having entered my brain, it was half an hour before I realized that by far the driest place to fish was underneath the bridge. I waded down through water that was up to my chest. By casting sidearm, I was able to fish the pool below the supports. Except for the pressure of the current on my back and the vibrations of lumber trucks ten inches above my head, it was like fishing indoors.

I was changing to a bigger streamer when I felt something slam into my waders above my hips—a log, as it turned out. We wrestled each other for a while, me trying to keep my balance, the log squirming like a little boy caught beneath my arm, spitting bark. I yanked on one of its branches and it pranced away downstream and vanished into foam.

"The trees are starting to go," my intellect said. It was very clear on that point. My instinct, though, still insisted on May.

"Three more casts," it said blindly. My intellect—scared witless now—said nothing.

I took a tentative step below the bridge. By leaning backward in the current as if I were hiking out on a sailboat, I somehow managed to keep my feet. It wasn't easy. The pounding water left me with something resembling vertigo. I felt I was teetering on the edge of a subway platform as the Seventh Avenue local roared by, in constant danger of being sucked in.

I was well past my three-cast limit when I became aware of a man in a yellow slicker watching me from beneath a pine tree on the bank.

"Water pretty cold, eh?" he said, displaying an even better Yankee twang than Ken's.

"Naw," I said. "Water's always nice in May."

But there was no fooling him. As he ducked around the pine tree his slicker opened far enough to reveal the uniform of a Vermont game warden.

"How's the fishing, sir?" he said, going to work.

"It stinks." I twisted around a bit so he could see the license pinned to my hat.

"Little rainy for fishing," he suggested. "Fact of it is, the river goes up another inch, highway department's going to close this bridge here. Won't be any getting east until it goes back down."

West of me were sixteen miles of flooded river, waterlogged trees that were beginning to tumble, dirt roads with no bottom, a car that started temperamentally in the rain. East of me was a warm pub with good Bourbon, my fiancée, a clean, well-lighted home. Getting out of that turgid water was the easiest decision of my life.

I talked with the warden as I packed my gear. He had been driving along the river intending to warn all the fishermen he met about the flood, but I was the only one he had found. Actually, he admitted with something like awe, I was the only fisherman he had seen in the last three days.

"Dedicated," he said, laughing.

"Stubborn," I said, putting him right.

As it turned out, the bridge held—the threatened flood never came. Still, there was enough rain throughout the rest of the week to make me consider all the alternatives to going back to that swollen river. The first was not to fish at all . . . Immediately rejected. Drastic measures were called for, but not that drastic. The second alternative was to head south for a drier Cape Cod and the "salter" streams I had fallen in love with when I lived there in the early '80s . . . Considered, then finally put aside. As beautiful as they are, those rivers formed a separate chapter in my life, and it would have been impossible to fish them without a heavy sense of *déjà vu.* The third was to fish a favorite trout pond in the New Hampshire mountains across the Connecticut . . . Attempted, then given up. Constantly bailing a leaky canoe has never been my idea of fun, and if any trout were rising while I was there, their circles were indistinguishable from those left by the rain.

So it was the river after all. There was a deeper reason for going back. This was the year I was devoting to the river alone, and I needed to stay in touch with it through all its moods, cranky as well as calm. As hard as its trout were to catch, the river itself—the sense of it—was even harder, and May was too soon to quit trying. There were occasional afternoons when the sun came out long enough to show what we were missing, and I would put away my writing and race the steaming shadows north. My fishing diary shows two rain-free hours on the 9th; three hours on the 12th; a whole afternoon on the 18th. As rare as the sun was, its effect on my face was galvanizing—I felt as if I had been switched onto solar, and the charge of energy was enough to last me through the inevitable change back to rain.

There was little chance of catching trout—the water was as high and thick as gravy in an overfilled tureen. But not catching trout is important, too. It opens up the fly fisherman to other moods and impressions, widens his focus from the small crescent of river swept by his fly. Troutless, we begin seeking alternate treasures to take home. Some might begin sketching or taking pictures of the river's scenery; some might use the time to reconnoiter parts of the river they don't already know. One woman I know picks up rocks along the river's edge, searching for fossilized nymphs; another goes into the woods in search of edible plants.

Me, I did none of these things. I opened up my ears and listened.

It would have been hard not to. A great deal of the river's energy was being expended in sound, and all my casts, all my journeys from stance to precarious stance, all my meditations, were backed by this roaring, rushing sweep. The aural power was intense—I felt as if I were in the middle of an amplifier, part of a circuit required for the sound's transmission. Overhanging branches strummed a whisking sound on the water racing beneath their tips; rocks clattered against each other like cymbals; boulders established a backwash of sound that was pitched to a slower, heavier rhythm than the current's main theme, a throb as ponderous and regular as surf.

The river had to raise its voice to get my attention. Like most fly fishermen, the sound of moving water has always been a pleasant accompaniment to my day—an *accompaniment*, little more than background noise, though of the loveliest kind. It had never occurred to me to try to analyze it. Sound's part in stalking fish, after all, is largely negative: we try to avoid making any. As a positive force, sound seldom enters our consideration. Fly fishing is primarily a visual sport—the finning trout and quick rise come to us through our eyes. Touch plays a part—there's the feel of the bottom as we wade, the pull on our line as a trout takes hold. Give up his sight or his sensation of touch, and the fly fisherman would be seriously handicapped; give up his hearing, and his skill would be reduced not at all.

Trout are partly to blame for sound's unimportance. They emit no beeping noises that help us locate them; they neither whistle, squawk, rattle nor hiss. A bubbly, splashing sound as they feed is the best they can do. Their dumbness is a curse and blessing both. It makes it harder for us to find them, but easier to fight them once we do. Would fly fishermen still enjoy catching trout if the fish could groan? "I hooked a noisy rainbow in fast water," we might say. "He ran out a hundred yards of line, screamed at the top of his voice, then took to the air . . . " No, somehow I don't think we would.

Between the trout's silence and the fly fisherman's unreliance on his ears, sound has not received the attention from fishing writers that it deserves. Like surf and wind, a river's rush is one of the elemental voices in which nature has chosen to speak. But the writers who are best at describing a river do it primarily in visual terms; we can see Haig-Brown's Campbell or Grey's Rogue, we can often feel them, but can we ever hear them?

Describing sound is not easy. The vocabulary of inanimate noise is limited. Things ring, pop, click, buzz, bang, creak, hum, clang, sizzle, squeak, and not much else. These are landbound, static words—they lack the dynamic flow liquid sound requires. Simile helps a bit; for instance, there's a small rapid below the Aquarium that makes a steady, sprinkly kind of sound, like the fountain on the terrace of Lincoln Center when it's turned on full blast. But while it is almost impossible to write about sound without such similes, they stand in the way. If we can only refer to a sound by relating it to other sounds, we sacrifice preciseness, put our words one or two steps beyond the sensations they're meant to describe.

A race of fishermen could easily invent a vocabulary to get around this. Take a sound that every fly fisherman knows well: water falling over a weir or small dam. It's a drumming, happy kind of sound, at least in English. In our angling vocabulary we could avoid all images of drums and happiness by giving it a precise name: *umshoo.* "I was fishing by the dam, listening to the river *umshoo,*" we could say, and fly fishermen everywhere would know what we meant. Water dropping over two or more weirs in succession would make a sound with one beat or more: *umshooeen.* Water running beneath an undercut bank would make a soft *squahish* noise . . . and so on.

Until such a language is adopted, fishing writers must rely on the similes on hand. Luckily, there is one vocabulary that is devoted pure and simply to describing variations in sound, and it fits a river quite well: the vocabulary of music.

A river's sound is nothing if not symphonic—one beautiful whole composed of scarcely less beautiful parts, each of which can be distinguished within the overmastering rhythm. The light, percussive effect of pebble hitting pebble; the reedy drone of sand washing away from a bar; the brassy fanfare of spray against granite . . . they weave their way in and out of the steadier, cello-like continuo of the river's motion. A river bed is a sounding board over which water strums the earth, shaking molecules against other molecules until a wave is formed which—reaching a certain frequency—reacts pleasantly on our ears. This scale established, the symphony begins.

A drop of water falls from a branch high upstream with a soft plucking kind of noise . . . solo at first, then joined by another drop further back toward the branch's stem, then another, then a fourth, until finally the pluckings become simultaneous, and the first liquid chord of the river is created—a high treble rill of sound as the merged raindrops sparkle down a grooved rock into the stream. The rain-formed current pushes a drowned branch against a boulder, then lets it spring back; pushes it, then lets it spring back, establishing a soft metronomic click from which the entire river takes its beat.

The character of the music is evident right from the start. The White River, for instance, is romantic even in its tributaries—a broad sweep of sound that suggests Smetena's *Moldau.* The Battenkill, running in a narrower channel, is more classical, a river composed by a Mozart or Haydn, with pure tones and an effortless harmonic impulse that carries you along.

My river in its upper reaches is unmistakably baroque. It begins far from the road in a quiet wood where silence is so absolute it seems not the mere absence of noise but a creative force waiting to be tapped. The instrumentation that gathers it is the simplest—there are those raindrops forming into rills, the baby tributaries with their high, brittle bounce, the miniature falls whose notes are as clear and distinct as a harpsichord's. With no heavy rapids to drown out their sound, the soloists retain their distinctness as the process goes on; close your eyes and you can still find the percolating drops of rain within the metallic, more ornamental notes of the falls. I listen to a Bach cantata by following one instrument or voice as it winds its way through the entirety of the piece, using it as a guide through the beautiful intricacy of sound, and I find myself listening to the upper stretches of my river in the same way.

Upstream, the sound is channeled into definite boundaries. Walk fifty yards from the banks, and the music is indistinguishable from the wind's. Below the first substantial tributaries, the sound widens and darkens—waterfalls add their bass notes and rapids pitch everything to a speedier tempo. Culverts give a hollow sound to the river; the supports of the highway bridges make a steely, atonal kind of noise that is out of synch with the river's lilt, giving the effect of an Ives forcing notes onto something by Schubert.

There's a rapid below the last bridge that makes a sound very much like human song—a delicate soprano voice struggling to be heard over the orchestration. The first time I fished there, I swore someone was calling my name from the bank. I turned to see who it was, but there was no one—the sound was coming from the rapid itself, as if there were a maiden entombed beneath the flow. How to account for it? Is there an underwater rock whose configuration mimics the human larynx? Is the rapid's pitch that of speech? Or is there a maiden entombed there after all, an Indian princess scorned by an early settler who took her life over the falls? Standing there listening to that unearthly whisper, it's easy to understand how myths begin.

Below this rapid, it's harder to separate the river's sounds into parts. I wade out to the rapid's edge to listen more attentively, but it's too close—there is a roar of white noise in which all kinds of boomings, skitterings, raps and gurgles lay concealed.

You have to go along with the sweep. With a river as with a symphony there comes a time when you have to stop trying to analyze it and let yourself be swept along in its sensuous beauty. By the time the South Branch comes in, the river's sound is at fullest amplitude, the various riffles, rapids, chutes and falls joining into one churning vibrato that becomes its own echo. A jet of water beats apart the muting bark of a log; a poorly balanced boulder rumbles sideways in the current, groaning Fs; a rapid sets up a sizzling noise as it drops shatter apart into spray; white, downpressing water drums furiously toward the bottom, then boils up again further downstream . . . all the river's effects are in chorus now, *allegro* now, then *presto,* joining together for one magnificent finale as the river gathers itself for that last percussive leap over the dam, a showy display of sound that is felt more than heard.

The invisible conductor of things brings his baton down, the last note fades away. The river makes a random, shuffling kind of noise in its last hundred yards to the Connecticut, like that of an orchestra's members going their own ways after the concert reaches its end. The river's undetectable currents finally merge. The flow out of silence into silence returns.

6

Take a Writer Fishing

∞

I dreamt one night that I was fishing with Joseph Conrad. We were on the open stretch of the river above the first bridge. I was casting a dry fly toward a shallow spot that couldn't possibly have held a trout; Conrad was shaking his head in disapproval, muttering something in Polish that I couldn't understand. He was fishing with a handline, hauling it in over his shoulder as if it were an anchor rope, really straining—his fine beard was drenched in sweat. I would have liked to help him, but was too shy. More than anything, I wanted him to approve of the river and love it as much as I did.

Too soon, he faded into Bob Cousy. But so vivid was his image that when I woke up that morning, I went to the library to determine whether there's any record of his having fished. Had I put him on that trout stream by myself, or was there some half-remembered reference to the sport buried away in *Nostromo?*

I suppose I'm to blame. None of the novels or stories contain fishing scenes, and there's no mention of any interest in his autobiographical writings. In the course of his maritime career he must have known men who fished hard for their living, and fishing for fun must have smacked to him of affectation.

Searching through Conrad, remembering the dream, I began trying to list all the great writers who are known to have been dedicated fishermen. It's a remarkably short list, and I'm not sure why. Is it

because great writers are too intellectual to take any interest in something so earthy as fishing? I don't think so—fly fishing has always attracted a brainy sort, and among its practitioners are a great number of scientists, engineers, artists and teachers. Is it because writers bear too complicated a burden of worry and concern to enjoy fishing's basic premise? This might be closer to it. Like any other human activity, fishing has its share of ironies, and perhaps the act of trying to fool a trout into thinking a piece of feather and steel is a mayfly is too fundamentally absurd for a great mind to endure... partly this, and partly that writers with their torments know too well what it's like to have a barbed hook in their throat, and have no wish to inflict the same torture on another harmless soul.

Let's go down the list. Hemingway is first, if for no other reason than that his love for fishing was the most self-advertised. The popular conception of Hemingway as a fisherman revolves around his days fishing off Cuba and the Keys on his beloved *Pilar*, with the kind of epic, day-long encounters with marlin that formed the basis of *The Old Man and the Sea*. While this kind of big-fish fishing, with its competitiveness, its emphasis on sheer physical power and machismo, obviously meant a lot to Hemingway and revealed much that was fundamental in his character, it doesn't present him in a particularly attractive light. Would it have been fun to be on the *Pilar* with him fishing the "great blue stream" of the Gulf? For a while, perhaps, then something of a bore. Arnold Gingrich, his friend and sometime publisher, claimed that "Ernest was a meat fisherman . . . intensely competitive about his fishing, and a very poor sport." This seems like an accurate appraisal; it's fun to catch a big fish, but not if your manhood is being measured by how fast you reel him in.

It's the younger, not-yet-legendary Hemingway—the Hemingway who fished grasshoppers for trout—who's the appealing one. The golden moments of his boyhood revolved around his trips to the lakes and streams of the Upper Peninsula of Michigan, the locale of his "Big Two-Hearted River." In this, and in his early journalism for the *Toronto Star*, there's a boyish sincerity and brightness that gives way to pontification twenty years later when he's writing about big game. Included in his early journalism are accounts of streams he'd visited in Canada and Europe, illuminated by the typically compact Hemingway style. Here's a man who can sum up the enchantments of a trout river in one beautiful phrase: "A pool whose moselle-colored water sweeps into a dark swirl and expanse that is blue-brown with depth and fifty feet across." Here's a man who has an eye for other things than trout, and can include in an account of a Swiss fishing trip meditations on barmaids in station buffets, Napoleon's army in the St. Bernard pass, and the latest news in a trout-stained *Daily Mail*. This Hemingway— the young man who hiked across the Black Forest in the '20s with a rucksack and a fly rod and not much else—is the one with whom I would have liked to fish.

Thoreau's another writer it would be fun going out on the river with, though you'd have to be prepared for some trouble. I don't mean dealing with his reserved personality (Sophia Hawthorne said that taking his hand was like taking the hand of an elm), but with his ambivalence toward fishing. Did he love it or hate it?

Read his account of night-fishing on Walden, and you'd swear no one ever loved the sport more. He tells of returning late to the pond from the village and spending the dark hours of midnight fishing from a boat, "communicating by a long flaxed line with mysterious nocturnal fishes . . . now and then feeling a slight vibration along it, indicative of some life probing about its extremity, of dull uncertain blundering purpose there, and slow to make up its mind."

Thoreau, for all his talk of simplicity, was too complicated a man to leave it at that. As much as he enjoyed fishing (we have that famous image of Thoreau playing the flute in his boat, charming the perch gathered about the bow), he was convinced that he *shouldn't*—that fishing, like hunting, was an important but essentially immature response to nature and its wonders, a pursuit for "embryo" man and not those attuned to the "higher laws." He puts down the fishermen who come to Walden thus: "They might go there a thousand times before the sediment of fishing would sink to the bottom and leave their purpose pure." He's equally hard on himself: "I have found repeatedly, of late years, that I cannot fish without falling a little in self-respect. I have tried it again and again. I have skill at it . . . but always when I have done I feel it would have been better if I had not fished . . . with every year I am less a fisherman . . . at present, I am no fisherman at all."

There's no apology at all in that other great nineteenth-century nature writer, John Burroughs. While Thoreau was at Walden deciding whether or not to fish, Burroughs was out on the Neversink, celebrating trout fishing with some of his happiest prose. "Trout streams coursed through every valley my boyhood knew," he writes in his essay, "Speckled Trout." He describes trips to the Delaware, Rondout, Beaverkill and Esopus—trips in which it was nothing for each fisherman to take a hundred trout.

Burroughs had more insight into the sport than Thoreau. He claims he'd seen more of woods and nature in "threading my native streams for trout," than he would have in any other way. Fishing "pitches one in the right key" to accept nature; the fisherman "is a kind of vagrant that nothing fears . . . all his approaches are gentle and indirect." With this attitude, fly selection is no problem: "When you bait your hook with your heart, the fish always bite!" And later: "A certain quality of youth is indispensable to the successful angler, a certain unworldliness and readiness to invest yourself in an enterprise that doesn't pay in the current coin."

Washington Irving fished some of those same Catskill streams. One of the essays in his *Sketch Book,* "The Angler," is a self-deprecatory account of his flirtation with trout. Reading Izaak Walton has left him "stark mad [about fishing] as was ever Don Quioxte from reading books of chivalry." Thus intoxicated, he ventures out on an upstate stream with all the necessary accouterments ("perplexed with half a hundred pockets") and begins to cast.

The results are meager. "For my part, I was always a bungler at all kinds of sports that require either patience or adroitness . . . I hooked myself instead of a fish, tangled my line in every tree, lost my bait, broke my rod and gave up the attempt in despair." Poor Irving! How we can sympathize with him! Nothing daunted, he ends the day reading his beloved Walton under the shade of a gentle oak. "There is certainly something in angling," he concludes, "if we could forget, which anglers are apt to do, the cruelties and tortures inflicted on worms and insects, that tends to produce a gentleness of spirit and a pure serenity of mind."

Irving's contemporaries were less fond of the sport. His friend Sir Walter Scott described himself as "No fisher, but a well-wisher to the game." He must have known a little about the subject; there's a scene in *Redgauntlet* where Darsie Latimer dismisses Charles Cotton's writings as not being applicable to Highlands streams, then goes on to spin his version of the familiar barefoot-boy-out-fishing–sophisticated-angler story. Scott's dismissal of Cotton is echoed in Lord Byron's put-down of Walton: "The quaint, old, cruel coxcomb in his gullet; should have a hook, and a small trout to pull it." Tennyson's poetry includes an occasional reference to fishing—apparently he shared with

Burroughs and Irving the opinion that it was good for the soul to engage in something so absolutely *uneconomic*. "Lusty trout to him were script and share; and babbling waters more than cent for cent."

To find the real angling poet you have to move ahead forty years to Yeats. It's funny about him. There's no mention of any fishing trips in his autobiography, and yet he wrote some of the finest poetry on the subject extant. There's "The Fisherman": "Although I can see him still,/The freckled man who goes,/To a grey place on a hill,/In grey Connemara clothes,/At dawn to cast his flies"; and "The song of Wandering Aengus": "Because a fire was in my head . . . I dropped the berry in a stream, and caught a little silver trout."

Reading Yeats, you come to the conclusion that what he really loved was the sound of the word *trout* and the pastoral, innocent image it conveyed. To him, trout were like fairies in the Irish hills—something you thought well of without actually wishing to catch. In all the fishing in print has there ever been a more magical line than the one from "The Stolen Child"? "We seek for slumbering trout, and whispering in their ears,/Give them unquiet dreams."

If Yeats is the epitome of the mystical fisherman, then Chekhov is the personification of the earthy one. No great writer ever loved fishing more. Nina, speaking of the writer Trigorin in *The Seagull,* could easily have been describing Chekhov himself. "And is it not wonderful that a famous writer, the darling of the public, mentioned daily in the papers . . . should spend his whole day fishing and be delighted because he has caught two chub."

Chekhov would have been a good man to fish with—caring nothing for orthodoxy, whether in literature or fishing, and with that rare ability to forget he's a great man. Fishing was a welcome diversion from the cares of literature and medicine; the moment he bought his country estate at Melikhovo in 1892, he began stocking his ponds with tench imported from Moscow in glass jars. Trigorin, the bemused writer stumbling about other people's lives carrying a notebook and a fishing rod, is in some part Chekhov's wry laugh at himself. (I once saw a performance of *The Seagull* in which Trigorin—a man fishing a farm pond for chub—carried the kind of huge saltwater rod Zane Grey might have used, thereby making ludicrous what was otherwise a fine production.)

Chekhov's real fishing masterpiece is a lesser-known story called "Fish." It bears the simplest of plots. Berasim, a peasant, is working by the river preparing a bathing shed when he grabs a huge fish that's hiding under some willow roots. Other peasants come over and offer their advice on how to land him ("But why do you keep poking with your hand?" cries the hunchback Lubim, shivering as though in a fever. "You blockhead! Hold him, hold him, or else he'll get away, the anathema! Hold him, I tell you!"); the matter isn't resolved until the master himself, Andrey Andreitch, hears the commotion and joins the fun.

"A famous eel-pout," mutters Yefim, scratching under his shoulder blades. "I'll be bound it weighs ten pounds."

"Mm . . . yes," the master assents. "The liver is fairly swollen! It seems to stand out! Aach!"

The fish makes a sudden, unexpected upward movement with its tail and the fishermen hear a loud splash . . . they all put out their hands, but it is too late; they have seen the last of the eel-pout.

It's all there—the simple excitement of it, the suspense, the climax and immediate anticlimax. Chekhov has always been regarded as the writer's writer, and based on the insights he shows in this story, he was the fisherman's fisherman as well.

T. H. White was another writer who had an uncanny insight into fish and fishing. We have that masterful scene in *The Sword in the Stone* where the Wart, the young King Arthur, is transformed into a tench by Merlin so he may swim about the castle moat and complete his education among the fish, nearly being swallowed by a pike in the process. White had a great natural affinity with animals, birds and fish; nature was a balm for the torments of his inner life, offering him the companionship he could never find with another human. White—with his falconer's patience—would have been a methodical fisherman and a learned one; he and Chekhov could have taught each other a lot.

With White, the list nears its end. (It could be extended by including contemporary fiction writers like William Humphrey, Caroline Gordon, Norman Maclean, Richard Brautigan and Tom McGuane, people who have written about fishing in imaginative and original ways.) Looking back on the writers mentioned, several names stick out by their absence—writers whose silence on fishing is in some ways a surprise.

Take Melville, for instance. Here's a man who in *Moby-Dick* gave us what is arguably the best "fishing" story ever written (Melville, remember, insisted that the whale was a *fish*), and yet there are only three or four vague references to fishing in his entire output, and they're all less than memorable. Take this poem from *Mardi:* "Fish, fish, we are fish with red gills/Naught disturbs us, our blood is zero/We are buoyant because of our bags/Being many, each fish is a hero . . . " Which is a long way from Yeats. But it's easy to understand why Melville wasn't a fisherman. To anyone who had clung to the sides of a whale boat on a Nantucket sleigh ride, catching ten-inch Berkshire trout must have seemed pretty tame.

Dickens is another novelist you might have expected to write about fishing, if for no other reason than he seems to have written about everything else. There are no anglers among his characters, not even among the sporting Pickwickians. Dickens does, however, hold an honorary place in the angling hall of fame. The Dolly Varden trout is named after the irrepressible Dolly Varden of *Barnaby Rudge,* "the very impersonation of good-humour and blooming beauty . . . giddy, flirtatious and coquettish."

Robert Frost should by rights be an angler. Of all the greats so far mentioned, he's the only one who might have known the rivers I love, and I regret there's no record in his poetry of any involvement. Ernest Poole, the novelist who was Frost's Franconia Notch neighbor, mentions in a reminiscence that Frost liked to go fishing in the spring, but these expeditions left no trace in his work. In his collected poems there is only one reference to fishing; it comes in "The Mountain" where the local farmer, in explaining his relationship to the mountain that rises behind his farm, says "I've been on the sides,/Deer-hunting and trout-fishing . . . " And that's it for Robert Frost. There are no hymns to New Hampshire trout streams, no recollections of fishing trips in the Green Mountains—his Hyla Brooks are always fishless. Like Conrad, he knew too well the hard work that went into wresting a living from nature to spare much attention to people who went to the woods for sport.

And what about William Faulkner? Why didn't he leave us a fishing equivalent of "The Bear"? He lived in a region where fishing was a way of life, and he must have listened to his share of fishing stories during his spell of purgatory at the local post office. Mississippi is bass country—the stories would have been of monster largemouths caught on frogs. And while these were kind of oral legends Faulkner thrived on, he never got around to writing as lovingly about fishing as he did about hunting.

There is one account of Faulkner's interest in fishing, and it's a poignant and moving one. After his death in 1962, his neighbors in Oxford put their recollections of the man they called Bill into a book. Among the contributions is one by J. Aubrey Seay in which he describes meeting Faulkner by a lake four days before the great writer's death. Seay was going fishing, and he asked Faulkner if he would like to come along. Faulkner politely declined—he wasn't feeling up to it—but he asked if he could sit and watch them fish through binoculars.

I've thought of that scene often lately—the great man bundled up against the death that was around the corner, staring out over the lake's surface with an old pair of binoculars, trying one last time to watch and learn. I think of Seay casting for bass from the bow of that boat across the lake—how fishermen can never know when they're posing for someone who might just possibly make them eternal. I picture myself on the river under that doomed, all-seeing gaze, and it makes me cast a little more carefully, doing everything in slow-motion so that Bill Faulkner—his hands trembling on the binoculars—can get it right.

7

June Sixteenth

∞

I teeter between two illusions when fishing. The first is apt to come on dark afternoons in early May when the river is so rain-swollen and muddy that even to think of casting into it seems an act of maddest optimism. No insects brighten the surface, no fry scoot from beneath my feet, and no trout intercept my streamer on its dull and hopeless course downstream. At these times I'm apt to conclude that acid rain, pesticides and hazardous waste have finished their poisonous work, leaving the river utterly fishless, devoid of life in any form.

My second illusion is the direct opposite. It consists of the absolutely unshakeable belief that there are fish in the river after all, and not only *in* the river, but that the very river itself is *composed* of fish, and that what normally would be taken for rushing water is in truth the speckled, iridescent backs of countless thousands of trout, rainbows and browns combining like hydrogen and oxygen in an elemental bonding. For a fly fisherman, this is a happier illusion. It makes fishing a much simpler chore, the taking of even a large trout being about as difficult as the act of dipping your hand in the water to drink.

I indulged in this second illusion once for fifteen-sixteenths of a perfect June day. The river, after being near flood stage for over a month, had settled into its proper springtime banks. The sogginess in the air was gone, swept out by a northwest wind that managed to combine the sharp clarity of fall with the lush promise of summer. The

farms along the river had roses growing in the marge of their fields. Baby lambs tripped over wildflowers; cows pranced as exuberantly as colts. Ten-year-olds, newly released from school, marched single-file through the meadows above the junction pool with butterfly nets, hunting for who knows what adventures in the tall and waving grass.

Me, I was fastened to a trout. It was the shady, narrow stretch above the cemetery, a part of the river I had never fished seriously before. As usual when searching new water, I had on a Muddler—a fly whose effectiveness and versatility make it a fine tool for probing. In confirmation of this, the fly was attached to the lip of a ten-inch rainbow who was bouncing out of the water below me as joyously and airily as spray. After a fishless month, I badly needed to feel him in my hand, and beached him more carefully than his size required. I held him in the current for several minutes before releasing him, partly to let him recover his strength, partly to re-establish my connection with the pulse of the river's life.

I had four more trout in the next eight casts—five if you count the miniature brookie I caught when I changed positions and let the line drag unattended behind me. Sometimes a river will come exactly into place with all its components—proper hatches at the proper times, perfect blendings of light and shade, optimum water level and temperature—and the fish will feed freely all day, as if compelled by the classic setting to do their part.

This is the kind of perfection I was wading through. By eleven, I had gone for the cycle—at least one rainbow, one brookie and one brown. It's not an uncommon feat on the river; the bright, native brookies tend to inhabit the upper stretches, but I have caught the paler stocked ones as far downstream as the dam, and the rainbows turn up everywhere. Brook trout are the natives here, of course, but in this part of the river there is a rootlessness about them that makes them seem like interlopers. I catch them in the riffles mostly, spots that are probably their second or third choice after the rainbow- and brown-usurped pools. It's a pathetic story, this—a hundred years ago, the river was entirely theirs. The human analogy would be the sons of farmers you see milling about the bars in New England towns, perpetual renters, their fathers' land gone to condominiums and malls.

There is a bit of this in the rainbows, too, as abundant and strong as they are. They're flashy and intelligent, these western transplants, but a bit much so for these quiet Vermont hills. When they zip across the river toward the west on the end of a line, I always imagine that they're trying, however forlornly, to get home.

It is the brown trout that seems most comfortable here. Why this should be so, I'm not sure, but I sense it every time I catch one. The brookies dash about in a semidisoriented way; the rainbows go airborne, but the German browns pull with the knowledge and power of successful imperialists. Just before noon, I took a fourteen-incher—on the river, my best brown by far—and he fought with what can only

be described as a supercilious air, running downstream with enough
hurry to let me know he was annoyed but not enough to betray any
anxiety. When I beached him, it wasn't because he submitted, but
because he was bored, and he swam off after his release with the
offended air of gentry compelled to argue with tradesmen over the
price of beef.

And so it went. I caught fish on whatever fly I tried—a yellow
Marabou, a Gold-Ribbed Hare's Ear, Matukas in three different
shades. The only thing that seemed to matter was the direction they
were fished; on a slow drift diagonally across the current, I could count
on a trout every third or fourth cast. There came to seem an
inevitability to it after a while. The line uncoiled and landed across the
river; the fly surfed for a moment on the lip of the current's edge; the
main, heavier current caught the belly of the line and pulled it under;
the fly swung in a long arc downstream; the line, just as it tightened
straight below me, tightened again, harder this time, as a trout took
hold.

The catching became a pattern, a consistency that seemed part of the
warp and weave of the day itself. This unfolding, scalloped arc of the
fly-line as it gradually swung downstream . . . it was hard not to believe
that this was precisely the dynamic geometrical line that nature had
picked to align itself on during that particular June day, and my success
with the trout was because—recognizing the grain—I had aligned
myself with it, too.

Number nine, number ten, number eleven. With each one, I came
to like this new stretch of river more and more. Vermont rivers, with
their infinite variation on the basic riffle-boulder-pool theme, have the
ability to suggest a great variety of other, more distant trout waters.
The hundred yards or so I was fishing is particularly rich in these
suggestions. Below me was a gravel bar that could have been right out
of the steelhead/salmon rivers that run down from the Olympics in
Washington. Behind me, the river narrowed enough for the willows in
either side to touch tops and form a tunnel, reminding me of forest
brook-trout water in Maine. The pool I was fishing now had the sandy
bottom you can find on the streams of Cape Cod, and the rapid beyond
it was as steep and tumultuous as any mountain brook in Colorado.

With a nice rainbow, I was up to a dozen, and it seemed like a good time for lunch. I climbed out of the river below the cemetery and walked over to the grass near its edge, sitting down only when I found a spot where the shade had my face, the sun my legs. Celeste had packed some sandwiches. I had been carrying a beer around in my wader pocket, and it was still satisfyingly cold.

Now it is hard to be near a cemetery sipping beer without doing some serious reflecting. What I mainly wondered about was whether anyone had ever written a treatise explaining why so many good fishing spots seem to be near cemeteries. I can think of half a dozen places off hand, and that's only in Vermont.

Is it because people avoid the area around a cemetery, thus ensuring that the pools there are underfished? Is it because our eighteenth-century ancestors had a lovely eye for terrain, and always picked out meadows to bury their dead, meadows that would be situated above placid, easy stretches of river? Is it because cemeteries with their calm, thoughtful air make the fisherman calm and thoughtful, too, thereby instilling the perfect attitude for taking trout? Or is it none of these things, but a mystic something that establishes communion between the ghosts of trout and fishers past with trout and fishers present?

I opened the gate to the cemetery to take a closer look. It's rectangular in shape, about an acre in area, with a gentle slope uphill from the river. Three sides are bordered by stone walls, the fourth by a strange Victorian version of a wire fence. With the sun at its highest, there was enough shade for all the graves—shadows cast by oaks that were saplings when the last burial there took place.

None of the headstones are dated past 1880—most are from a time far earlier. Roughly half are the same four-foot height, simple and unadorned, but here and there one rises above the others where a family had indulged in some morbid one-upmanship. (Seeing them, one can picture the conflict in the eighteenth-century Puritan mind between the need to show that dear departed whoever was no better than anyone else and the belief that he or she *was* in fact better, and thus deserved a *slightly* higher headstone.) The only truly extravagant one features a scowling man in what's apparently meant to be a toga, towering above his headstone with one finger gravely raised to heaven like the

Commendatore in *Don Giovanni.*

Efforts had been made to keep the cemetery neat, but the grass hadn't been cut in weeks and several of the headstones had tipped over. There was yellow lichen growing in the inscriptions—it was only by kneeling down and squinting that I could make out the words.

There are some real patriarchs buried in that little grove. Phineas S. Cobb, for example, who died February 27, 1832, aged 74; a Revolutionary War veteran who would have been eighteen in 1776, old enough to be with Johnny Stark's men down at Bennington. Not far from him lies Susannah Thompson, who died September 20, 1859, aged 93—a lifespan that took her from the time Vermont was an unexplored wilderness to the eve of the Civil War.

Some of the headstones are tragic reminders of a time when parents routinely outlived most of their children. Thus, "Freeman J. Claflin, Died Dec. 24, 1831, Aged 1 Year 7 Months 21 Days," or below it, "William W. Claflin, Died Nov. 25, 1831, Aged 20 Days." Picture that hideous winter in the Grant home. The baby dead first, just when the trauma of birth was over and he had begun to be dear to them all, then the other boy, down with perhaps the same flux or cough that had taken the baby, dead Christmas Eve.

Some of the headstones have poetry that is still legible, including Esther Loop, who in 1852 was addressed as follows: "Thus Like the Sun, slow Wheeling to the Wave;/She sank in Glory to her welcome Grave." Others are unintentionally funny. The last headstone I read marked the final resting place of a Wealthy A. Flint and her husband, Worcester T. One can picture the charming old fellow, a character out of Dickens as played by W. C. Fields.

When I returned to the fishing, it was with the feeling that I knew a little more about the river and the valley and my place in it. The sun had gotten around the trees now, and there was a sheen on the water that seemed as liquid and real as a second, higher river superimposed over the first. I caught my thirteenth trout of the day on my first cast, and within half an hour was up to fifteen.

Fly fishermen insist that it is quality, not quantity they are after, but even so most of us go around with a figure in our head that represents our own personal high. Mine is fifteen trout caught and released—tied several times, but never broken. I've come to think of it as a psychological barrier, a limit beyond which sport veers toward greed. The truth is that by the time I've caught even ten trout, I'm sated, and any further catching seems repetitive and dull. Even worse: at ten, a fisherman can pat himself on the back, pride himself on his skill; at fifteen, it's easy to believe that skill has no part in it at all, and that even Wealthy A. Flint herself, dead these ninety years, could catch her limit.

Still, it was too nice an afternoon to quit—I saw no harm in raising my record one more notch to sixteen. About twenty yards upstream, the river divided itself around a small island; the channel closest to the bank spilled over a large, flat rock into a pool the size of a card table. There was a trout there and a good one—I could make out his back beneath the competing swirls of sunlight.

By crossing to the lower end of the island, I could drop a fly over him without any problem. Once hooked, he would speed down the pool into the main current where I would have room to control his runs. Checking off number sixteen in my head, I tied on a nymph.

So far, so good. What I've forgotten to mention, though, is what I had forgotten to take into account: a water-smoothed log jutting obliquely out of the water in the pool's center, as sharp and menacing as a tank trap. There was no way around it. I could wade upstream and fish from above, but the river shallowed out before the pool, and there wouldn't be room to get the necessary swing in my drift before the fly grounded on the island. Even if I did hook him from above, his first run would inevitably carry him around the log, dooming my leader.

I started thinking. Maybe not a nymph after all—maybe a small Hendrickson dry. But no—there weren't any Hendricksons hatching. Perhaps a Quill Gordon instead. A Quill Gordon, or maybe an Adams.

I ended up using all three. My first cast brought a rise, but a half-hearted one, and when I struck at his shadow, the fly snapped back into my face.

Fine. A little more determined now, I went to the Muddler—for the trout, the kiss of death.

"Sixteen, you're mine," I said to myself, working the fly out so it would drop a little shy of the log.

If I listed all the flies I left sticking out of that wretched log in the next hour, you would have a complete inventory of my fly boxes; if I described all the different positions I cast from, you would be bored. The upshot, of course, was that I didn't catch that fish. No more rises, not even a quiver of interest as the occasional fly bumped his nose. By the time I gave up trying for him, the other fish had stopped taking, too. In the shreds and patches of my illusion, it seemed as if the trout-composed water had evaporated into dusk.

I was mad for a while, damned mad, but reflecting on it now, I realize that this last uncatchable trout was the most important fish of the day. The balloon of my pride had been expanding all afternoon, and the trout had been the gentle agent of its puncture. My sated, smug feeling was gone, replaced by the puzzled yet hopeful attitude a fly fisherman should never lose.

Next time, I would deliberately cast a small Bivisible *across* the log, letting it swing down like a pendulum left to right, teasing him, until . . .

Next time, I vowed as I climbed out of the river. Next time, trout. Next time!

Which—when you stop to think about it—is the nicest gift a fish can give.

8

Dusk into Dark

∞

The past is often compared to the twilight, but what about comparing the twilight to the past? It has that remoteness to it. In July, when the sky at nine is three faint shades from the most delicate orange, it has that remoteness. It has the finished quality of the past, the sense that nothing essential can any longer be added or removed. The moving hand, having writ, moves on; the sun, having warmed the day and glorified its last few seconds, moves on. The past's serenity is reproduced in its setting. Watching it, the hurry in us dissolves, vanishing into a spacious sense of well-being and completeness that mirrors the dusk's calm. Anxiety can't touch it. It is the only moment in the world's long day that demands a single response: peace.

And so I fish it, staying as close as I can to its edge.

Edge. It's difficult to pin down. Put simply, it's the dividing line between dusk and dark, the light remaining between the moment the sun disappears beneath the horizon and the moment when it is finally night. The first limit, of course, is charted and fixed. In Vermont, summer sunsets are around nine, though fragments of blue and white may persist in the sky for another hour. This makes the other limit of the edge, the dark, much harder to determine. Is it when the soft pink is gone over the western hills? Is it when the fly fisherman can no longer see his fly riding on the river's surface? When he can no longer see his line?

This last is closer to it. There comes a moment when casting begins to lose its measured rhythm and the fly fisherman senses he is beginning to lose control. The fly shoots back dangerously close to his forehead; the leader, lost in half-light, refuses to uncoil. Hooks become unthreadable. Rocks once safely dormant spring to life—malevolent rocks that reach out a gritty edge to trip us. There is a hurry in our fishing that is all the more dramatic for its contrast to the preceding minutes of calm. One moment the fly fisherman is the picture of civilized grace; the next, he's a caveman caught in the nether world far from fire. This loss of control—this sensation of entering another realm where our power is dramatically reduced—is the essence of night and its only true boundary.

Put it at 9:40 or 9:45. The half-hour that comes before is my favorite time to fish in the summer. I have a redhead's sensitivity to the sun, and the intense light of July afternoons makes me as prickly and shy as a vampire. Fly fishing at night is something I'm ambivalent about at best. It is dusk when I am most comfortable, the brief period when enough sun is gone to cool the river, but enough is left to light it.

It can be a magic time. The haze of daylight is gone, liberating a coolness that was latent in the earth all along. Our sense of hearing becomes more acute as the power of our eyes declines, and sounds that were merged into undifferentiated background noise become separate and distinct. A church bell in the distant village chimes the hour. Firecrackers left over from the Fourth pop harmlessly over the hills. Birds sing with the enthusiasm and purity they had at sunrise; a whippoorwill starts up in that always vague, undetectable locale that is the bird's domain.

Casts become like brush strokes. This cast upstream toward the center of the willow-draped pool is a quick stroke of red, spun downstream toward you with a last decorative splash of pink; this cast quartering toward the far bank, a stroke of purplish-black that bleeds into sky.

Is it the shortness of twilight that gives it such richness? I remember flying out to Colorado once—how for an hour or more the plane kept pace with the sunset, and the horizon retained the same underlining of orange. It was dusk, but not real dusk; without fading it carried no regret, no ending, and lost half its beauty for that reason.

I wonder if trout are saddened by it. It's a facetious question, but I wonder all the same. Does the gradual blackening of the water above their lies make them think back on their days as fingerlings, regret mating partners they've lost track of, make them sense their mortality? Dusk must be a great disturbance for them, faced as they are with a dramatic change in the elemental lighting through which they swim. If trout were ever prone to introspection, surely this would be the time.

If there is a caddis hatch on, they're probably too busy feeding to think about anything at all. In a pool like the Aquarium, they will be everywhere, splashing the water apart as if to fan it back to light. Their hurry can be contagious. Instead of contemplating the sunset smoking his pipe, the fisherman is casting toward the rises in a frantic, beat-the-clock sort of way. It's the hatch you want to keep pace with, the insects' urgency, and a trout actually caught at dusk can seem like an interruption.

The interesting fish are the ones that lead you *over* the edge. I was fishing the stretch below Jonathan Sharp's dairy farm—the stretch with the Sphinx-sized boulders—and about fifteen minutes after the sun disappeared, hooked a good trout. At first, the fight went all my way. I tightened on him quickly, managed to hold my rod high enough to keep the line disentangled from the boulders, and had no trouble chasing after him along the bank. If anything, I was too casual about it. Between one moment and the next, dusk was into dark and the equation had drastically changed. The trout could see exactly where he was going, whereas I had begun to stumble. It was no contest—the trout's night senses were better evolved than mine, and on his next run past the bank, he twirled the line around a boulder and broke free.

He had taken me into night and left me there—blind, lost and angry. I had absolutely no idea what to do next.

It's strange about fishing at night. Not too long ago, I would have told you that it was my favorite time to be out on the water, but this was when I was fishing lakes for bass. There are all kinds of lights and landmarks on a lake, and the reassuring presence of the boat acts as an axis on which you can orient your senses.

This is not the case when fishing a river. You're on your feet *in* the river, and there's never any telling what the next step will bring. Landmarks are few. On narrow stretches, the trees form a dome, blotting out the stars. Even if you're on a section of the river you know intimately, the dark has a way of distorting features until your very knowledge works against you. Ah, a big flat rock. Then surely I must be above the junction pool. But how could I have gone that far? I must have gone by it. Perhaps there are other flat rocks?

The mind becomes snarled.

I have been fishing at night all month, and I still can't master it. There are world-class rock climbers who can never go to the Himalayas because something in their physiology can't take altitude. Is it the same with fly fishermen? Are there some whose senses don't have that night adaptability, that mysterious blend of touch, sight and hearing that only comes into play when light is gone?

Deeper yet. Is fly fishing all wrong at night, a misplaced conceit? If we use the fly rod as a means of becoming more intimately involved with the river, then perhaps it is. Intimacy does not lie in flailing the water with badly timed casts, nor is it found in stumbling blindly over rocks. The problems night-fishing presents are those of navigation, not presentation, and the less bother your tackle is, the more you can concentrate on this fundamental task. A worm on a bent pin would be best. Against the mystery of night, anything else is ostentation.

Consider the problems. Here I am again in that meadow below Jonathan Sharp's night-grazing cows. It is 10 o'clock on a perfect Vermont summer night. I would like very much to enter the river, but I can see no way down the steep and slippery bank (a flashlight is cheating; if you fish at night, fish *in* night). Even if I find a path, I have no idea where the pools are that hold trout. Should I locate one, I will have trouble fishing it, since the absence of a clear horizon makes me mistime my casts. Even if I straighten these out, I still have no idea what fly to use. Dry flies are useless if you can't see them; I've read about hooking trout by sound, but it's clearly impossible—there are too many other slurps, trickles and plops around to distinguish a quiet sip. I could fish a sunk fly, but not without hang-ups; I've lost over forty flies this month—in tree limbs, earlobes and bat wings. But what difference does it all make? If I hook a fish, I'll have no way of following his fight and he'll break off anyway . . . Here I remain in the meadow beneath Jonathan Sharp's night-grazing cows.

I'm sure there are answers to all these dilemmas—the hell of it is, I can't find them. I've consulted my library of fishing books, but without much luck. Fishing for trout after dark was illegal in most states until fairly recently, and there is no tradition of night-fishing lore to draw upon—no Gordon to seek advice from, no Bergman. The only book I found that had much to say about the subject was Lawrence Koller's *Taking Larger Trout.* Don't use conventional flies, he says; lull the fish into a false sense of security, and keep your fly in the water at all times. "In all night operations for trout, the emphasis is on constant casting, quiet movement and slow fishing."

Okay, Mr. Koller. But doesn't constant casting contradict slow fishing? And exactly how am I going to lull the fish into a false sense of security? If anything is real and unshakeable in my river at night, it's the trout's security—there's nothing false about it.

Out of ten nights' fishing this month, I've caught only one trout. I was wading through the moonlight above the pine canyon last week. I had stopped to examine something there in the water (it was a branch, but I thought at first it was the skeleton of a dead trout), when my line suddenly tightened. This is it! I thought. Night-fishing's balleyhooed reward—the monster brown that feeds only at dark. But alas, it wasn't he. It was a four-inch brookie, the smallest trout I've taken all year.

I'm staying out late again tonight. As discouraging as the process has been, there have been aspects of it that I've enjoyed. The light of the moon on the water, the way the current ripples it into overspreading little waves, the scalloped Vs that resemble a child's drawing of gulls, only in silver; the flickering yellow beams of kerosene lights on farmhouse porches through the trees; the quick, illuminating arc of a headlight thrown across the river as a car negotiates a bankside curve; the distant haze of stars; the new mysteries night brings to familiar water . . . all these things will continue to lure me out, and in the course of the summer I may begin to catch a sense of what night-fishing is all about.

Until that time, dark will always be a limit—my favorite time on the water will continue to be dusk. Not day, not night, but the peaceful edge of beauty in between.

9

A Trout for Celeste

∞

F or me, fly fishing and fly fishing alone have always been synony-
mous. Out of the several hundred times I've gone trout fishing in
the last ten years, I can only think of two occasions when someone
went with me, and these were both very recently. Being alone has
become as much a part of my fishing as the river's current—a constant
push of solitude, sometimes destructive, sometimes soothing, but
always there.

Solitude has always seemed to me an enormous force. At various
times I have cursed it, longed for it, used it, feared it, lost it and found
it again. What I have never done, though, is understand it. Thus, it's
difficult for me to account for the strange gaps solitude has created in
what's otherwise been a reasonably gregarious life. I write fiction for a
living, yet I've never met another novelist; I like opera, yet know no
opera fans. So too with fly fishing. Having loved it as much as I have,
having pursued it with such attention, you'd think I would have
enjoyed many rich friendships based on a mutual love of the sport,
garnered many fine memories and anecdotes about my friends. I have
none of these, and envy those who do. A friendship made on a trout
stream must be a precious thing, almost as precious as solitude itself.

As solitude itself. I put it that way deliberately, because it's an
accurate description of the way I once felt. Right from the start the
memories that meant most to me in fly fishing were those of being

71

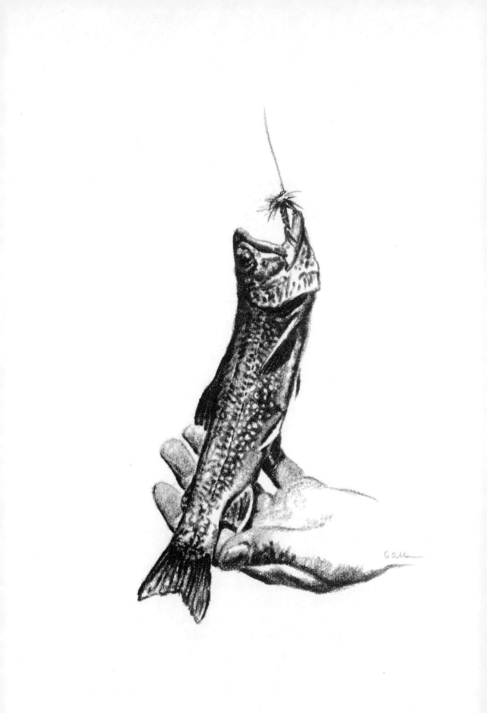

alone with the river and the fish. I can remember a September day on Cape Cod's Quashnet when I fished upstream into a setting sun—how the river seemed the sun's emanation, a narrow path leading into the secret heart of things, wide enough for one traveler alone. I remember an April afternoon on the Battenkill when the river was so high I had no business being in it, and how as I fought to stay upright, fish suddenly began rising on all sides, so freely and willingly that it seemed I was being initiated into their presence, made—in recognition of my daring—an honorary trout. Closer to home, I can think of dozens of times when I uncased my rod along the river feeling the kind of bitterness about my writing that verges on tears, then returned after an hour alone feeling calm and whole again, ready to work no matter what the cost . . . . All these things solitude has given.

It would be wrong not to total up the debit side as well. Not having anyone to go fishing with has probably made me less adventurous than a good fly fisherman should be; there are remote trout ponds I've had to pass up because they require too much hard bushwhacking to do alone, distant rivers that require too much driving. Then, too, my fishing education has proceeded more slowly than it would have if I'd had a fly-fishing friend to learn from, my store of experience to draw upon when selecting a fly reduced by at least half. I would dearly love to watch a good nymph fisherman in action, for instance; I've tried to teach myself how to do it, but without someone to study, it's been frustratingly hard.

Two serious demerits. But I think what I have lost most by my solitude is the companionship of another memory and perspective, someone to recall for me events and scenes that have long since slipped away. We're all aware of the marvelous moments that can come between friends who haven't seen each other for a long time—how your friend will mention an incident that you had completely forgotten, making you smile in discovery and delight, as if recovering a lost, precious jewel you only at that moment realized you owned. I remember that sunset on the Quashnet and that hatch on the Battenkill, but there are other events of those days that are beyond my recall, and it would mean much to me to have someone else who had shared them—a keeper of one-half the memory who had reflected on and preserved a portion of an experience that can at times seem too beautiful and vast for one imagination to hold.

Solitude, in other words, came to seem an enchanted castle half-deliberately created, to be longed for at some times, escaped from at others. The problem with erecting castles, though, is that they can become too real to be lightly given up, their ramparts too thick to be conquered by even the warmest of affections. *Wanting* to fish alone is one thing, but *having* to fish alone is something else, and I had begun to wonder whether I had crossed the line. With a decade's solitude at my back, had it become so precious to me that I couldn't relinquish it? Not be able to go fishing with anyone else without foaming at the mouth, throwing rocks at their fish and in general acting like an unsociable hermit? Exactly how high had those castle walls become?

Not too high, thank God. The ramparts have come tumbling down and the heroine who bid them fall is as intelligent and beautiful a princess as any fairy tale ever boasted. How Celeste entered my life is outside this essay's bounds, but what is important is the total unexpectedness of it. I was thirty when we met, at the age when friends start referring to you as a confirmed bachelor.

"I am waiting for the perfect woman," I would say, in response to their teasing. "She will emerge out of the woods one morning equipped with a backpack, a fly rod, a tape deck with Jussi Bjoerling on it, a Newfoundland puppy and a well-thumbed copy of Melville's *Pierre.*"

Celeste came unencumbered with any of these things, but what she does possess is infinitely more dear—a complete willingness to blend her enthusiasms with mine. We shared fishing right from the start. It wasn't fly fishing, not yet, but the kind of random trolling I used to do with my Dad. We'd drive over to one of the big Vermont lakes and rent a boat, cruise in big loops along the shoreline, talk about every subject imagination can hold. There were muskrats to play tag with, beaver and seagulls and geese. Celeste, being French, has determined notions about what a good picnic lunch should include, and we had some real feasts as we drifted lazily there in the sun.

Celeste hooked her first fish on Lake Champlain in May. It was probably a bass, and I say probably because I was so excited for her that

I nearly fell out of the boat in my anxiety to reach the engine and shut it off. Celeste was just as excited as I was—there was a lot of yelling, a lot of wild balancing to keep the boat from tipping over, then a moment of sudden and utter dejection when we realized the fish was gone.

No matter. A hundred yards up the shore she had another bite. Through a superhuman effort of self-control, I managed to stay where I was in the bow, and she landed it herself: a fine smallmouth bass of almost two pounds. As I write, I can look up at the wall and see their picture—the bass looking sleek and strong; Celeste holding him with a big grin on her face, the same irresistible grin I've seen in photos of her taken when she was five.

She followed up this first success with a landlocked salmon on Lake Willoughby. Once again I nearly managed to blow it for her. We were trolling, and I kept insisting that she let out more line. Celeste, trusting my advice, let out line even when I didn't tell her to, until her Dardevle was a good 150 yards behind our boat.

"Hey, there's a salmon!" I yelled, pointing toward the far side of the lake. It was jumping, and I couldn't understand why.

"My rod!" Celeste screamed.

The tip was bouncing wildly up and down. Still, I couldn't see the connection—the salmon was simply too far away to be hers.

Celeste's naiveté won her the fish. She began cranking the reel as if the salmon *was* hers, and to my complete amazement it was. After a ten-minute struggle, she had him alongside the boat, just in time for me to realize I had left the landing net back in the car. I grabbed the salmon as firmly as I could by the tail . . . For a moment I had him in my hands . . . He gave a convulsive twist and was gone.

Celeste looked at me with an expression that managed to combine suspicion, hope, anger and trust.

"You got him!" I said, putting the best light on it I could.

"But I wanted to hold him!"

"Well, we were going to let him go anyway. But as long as we touch him, it counts."

"I can tell people I caught a salmon?"

"Sure. As long as one of us touches him, like I said."

Which is a pretty liberal interpretation of landing a fish. We've adopted it as a rule now; flexibility in logic makes fishing with Celeste a joy.

Having shared these things with Celeste, the next step was to bring her to the river I loved. I was fishing it three and four times a week, coming back at night with all kinds of stories. It was funny about these. I talked like she knew the river as well as I did; we shared so many other things, I felt as if by a natural osmosis she should have absorbed my knowledge of the river, too, even though I had never taken her there.

My stories all ended the same way. "Someday you'll have to come with me."

"Okay."

And we left it at that. For a while, it was a satisfactory compromise—Celeste was sharing some of my fishing, but I was left with my precious solitude. The river was still my secret place—not *for* me as much as *in* me, and Celeste sensed it too well to intrude.

I'm not sure when the turning point came. As our relationship deepened, I began looking at the river in a different way. Before, I had always taken in its beauty as something to be hoarded, used in some future translation—a book perhaps, or simply a memory. Now though, I was trying to see the river through her eyes, imagine what her response would be to its multivarious forms. A trout finning easily in an eddy below a rock; a heron gliding in for a landing on a quiet pool; a coil of silver water swirling over sand—these were my secrets, and between one cast and the next I wanted more than anything to share these secrets with her.

"Someday you'll have to come with me," I said one night, describing the heron.

"Okay."

"How about tomorrow afternoon?"

Celeste looked at me carefully. "Okay," she said.

That easily can a decade's habit disappear. I won't describe every moment of our day. I didn't foam at the mouth, or throw rocks at the fish or feel violated. We fished the pine canyon, then the Aquarium, then the South Branch—having waited so long to share the river with her, I wanted to cram as much into our afternoon as possible, and I raced her madly from pool to pool.

In one of the last I caught a trout for her—a rainbow who took my bucktail near the surface and put on a melodramatic display, with extravagant leap after extravagant leap, as if he were showing off for her just as much as I was. How macho we both were! There is nothing more satisfying to the male ego than catching a trout for the woman you love, and when I beached it, I laid it at her feet like a knight at a tournament, waiting for her decision.

"Let's keep it," she said in delight. Then, seeing its beauty: "No, let's put it back."

I handed her the rod after that, and showed her the first steps in casting a fly. She made all the beginner's mistakes—whipped the rod back and forth too fast, tilted it sideways at the wrong angle to the water—but beneath the awkwardness was a rhythm and grace that promised great things for the future. I called out advice at first, but that was tactless, and after a while I was content to sit there on the bank and watch her puzzle things out for herself.

We stayed until late in the afternoon, started to leave, then decided to stay a little while more. There was a sunset to share with her—cooling shadows and the evening hatch . . .

We shared the fishing now, and we shared the river, but there was a third, missing step in the equation: Celeste still hadn't caught a trout.

It wasn't any trout she wanted. Listening to my stories, examining the pictures in my books, she decided her first trout should—no, must—be a brook trout.

"What's wrong with a brown?" I said.

"Brook trout are prettier. They're like maple leaves."

"Maple leaves?"

"They're part of Vermont."

Now there are at least four streams within five minutes of us that contain brook trout, and it would probably have taken a half-hour of lazy effort to fulfill her goal. There was a problem, though: our wedding. It used up all our free time for a month. True, we were going out west for our honeymoon, but that naturally meant a cutthroat or rainbow for her first trout, not a brookie.

We flew to Seattle and rented a car. The Olympics were first. We spent so much time hiking, climbing and beachcombing that fishing had to take a back seat, which in a strange kind of way was all right with me. I found the rivers so beautiful that I was half afraid to go near them, fearing that once under their spell I could never leave. We did fish the Skokimish for an afternoon, and then later the Quinault, but only briefly, and without catching anything. The day before we were due to fly back home we were in Mt. Rainier, and we decided to have one last try.

It was an eerie time to be there. A cloud had settled on top of the mountain, and everything above four thousand feet was draped in fog. At Paradise, the parking lot was filled with bewildered tourists groping around trying to find the lodge, only a few yards away. A ranger had been dispatched to help everyone. We asked about the fishing, and he recommended hiking into Mystic Lake—there were plenty of trout there, some running to size.

I pointed at the map. "What about this Snow Lake?" It was on the trail beyond Mystic, higher and more remote.

"It's pretty," the ranger agreed, "but it's sterile. There are no fish in there at all."

Mystic Lake it was then. Driving at a crawl, we finally located the trailhead. It was good weather for hypothermia—damp, in the low fifties—and I suddenly had this great desire to end our trip with a celebratory glass of Bourbon back in the Paradise bar. Celeste, though, already had her climbing boots on, and was starting resolutely up the trail.

The mist grew thicker the higher we climbed. There were wildflowers along the trail, but it was all we could do to make them out. According to our map, Mystic Lake was a mile and a half uphill, but we walked much further than that without spotting it, and the pond we finally came to had a sign that read Snow Lake.

The ranger was right about its beauty. All we could see of it in the mist was the outlet—a jumble of water-burnished logs under which the lake funneled itself into a stream—yet it was enough to suggest the wild, remote beauty of the whole, just as the glories of a string quartet may lie implicit in its first brief phrase.

We balanced our way out to the thickest of the logs, and sat down to eat lunch. A few hikers came by. Seeing our rods, they told us what we already knew: the lake was completely fishless. We decided to wait for a while to see if the fog would lift enough for pictures, then head back down to Mystic to fish.

In the meantime, strange things were happening. Something flew past my head and I swatted at it, without really sensing what it was. A moment later, a second something drifted by. I was ready for the third: a big brown mayfly, newly hatched.

Without saying anything to Celeste, I scrambled across the logs to get a closer look at the water above the logjam. Out there in the mist, so faint and fragmentary I thought I was hallucinating, were rings. Ripples against a rock, I assumed; but no—they were breaking across the surface at irregular intervals.

Curiouser and curiouser.

"Know something?" I said, turning around.

Celeste looked up from the map. "What?"

"There are trout in this lake."

She didn't believe me. Still, once she saw me casting, she came over and started fishing, too, more to humor me than anything else.

"There aren't any trout in this lake," she grumbled, only "lake" became a two-syllable word—lake as the first syllable, a scream of delight as the second.

"I've got one!"

A fish had plucked her fly off the surface just before it drifted into the logjam, hooking itself. It was a bad place to play one, and Celeste in her excitement stripped in line too fast, but it was exactly the right tactic—once into the logs, her leader would have been doomed.

Snow Lake never heard such happy shouts. Celeste had the fish dancing by our log now. Using my hat as a landing net, I knelt down and scooped him up, pressing him to my chest so he wouldn't squirm away. It wasn't until we reached the safety of shore that we dared to look at him.

"What kind is it?" Celeste asked.

I kissed her. I couldn't stop laughing.

"What kind!" she demanded.

"Celeste, you have just caught yourself a dyed-in-the-wool, authentic, bona fide . . . brook trout!"

Three Vermonters and there we were, two and a half thousand miles from home. They must have been stocked there, I explained—probably some program that was started with all kinds of hope, then abandoned for lack of funds. It was a long way to go to catch our neighborhood trout, but no matter—Celeste had her fish story now, and the adventure of it sealed our sharing.

"Take our picture!"

And I did, and as I focused the lens, the fog lifted, and behind her I saw the snowbanks and glacier and cliffs that framed the pond, revealing themselves only now when the moment was perfect. I held the camera steady until the beauty of the water and the woman and the trout came together, then—the moment captured—I crossed over the logs and took my wife by her hand.

10

The One That Got Away

∞

Wariness is among the prime Vermont virtues, but it is not among mine. I have not had to cope with the maddening swings of New England weather for an entire lifetime, I have never tried to pry a living from its soil, and my formative years were not spent among a people whose first, instinctive reaction when faced with any dilemma or choice is to do nothing.

Still, wariness is a quality I could use a little more of, particularly during August's low water. Take yesterday, for example. I had every intention of making a lazy day of it. Breakfast at the diner, a leisurely drive to the river, then some unhurried casting for some unhurried trout.

It was all a trick, of course. By lulling myself into a relaxed mood, I was hoping to surmount my usual abruptness, the better to catch trout that were bound to be as wary and uncoaxable in the summer sunlight as the oldest farmer in these hills.

I got out of bed as cautiously as though the fish could see me; I shaved and showered as quietly as I could. Breakfast was slowly and deliberately chewed, coffee daintily sipped—if I was going to spook any trout today, it wouldn't be in the diner. I drove the few remaining miles to the river more slowly than usual, and even went so far as to stop when I passed the farm with the hand-lettered sign: GOOD JUNK CHEAP!

Now, I am not a tag-sale freak, though I'm related to people who are (the date of our wedding had to be changed because there was a tag sale on the common outside the church on the same day, and we seriously wondered whether half the guests, given the choice between second-hand junk and a wedding, might not choose the junk). I will stop, however, if I see some books; for the past couple of years, I've been on the lookout for those two gentle classics of Vermont fishing, Frederick Van de Water's *In Defense of Worms,* and Murray Hoyt's *The Fish in My Life.*

There was a dilapidated Ping-Pong table on one side of the yard; sugaring barrels and old crocks on the other. In between were card tables and boxes piled high with stuff—muffin pans, headless dolls, old milk bottles, the works. Behind the wobbliest table stood a woman in her fifties who seemed as battered and used as any of her goods. Before her was a sign that read NO REASONABLE OFFER REFUSED, but there was a suspicious, hard-looking quality in her expression that let you know she had very strict notions about what that word "reasonable" meant.

As usual, the books were all romances, and I had turned to leave when I noticed something jutting out from the bottom of the midden heap on the Ping-Pong table. I'm still not sure what caught my eye first—the soft brown fabric of the cloth sleeve or the bright silver ferrule exposed above it.

Slowly, doing nothing to betray my interest, I worked my way across the yard, being careful to examine all the miscellaneous junk that intervened. The stuff on the table was high enough to block the woman's view; kneeling, I peeled the sleeve down far enough to see that it contained a bamboo fly rod, and a good one. The inscription near the butt was worn off, and only one letter was legible, the letter *L. L,* I decided, as in Leonard.

Eureka. Still, I wasn't going to blow it now. With a tremendous force of will, I left the rod where it was and made a circuit of the other tables, doing my best to seem disinterested and bored. Five minutes went by. When I turned to go back to the rod, a man with a complexion like cheap corduroy was waving it back and forth in his hands.

Where had he come from? I looked back toward the driveway. A purple Lincoln Continental with Jersey plates was parked there with its motor running, three kids crammed in the back. I cursed myself, then went back over to the crocks to await developments.

The man wiggled the rod back and forth for a while, bent it, whipped it about some more, then with a "why not?" kind of shrug, took it over to the woman.

"Four dollars," she said.

I could have strangled her. A Leonard in that kind of shape (and I was convinced in my frustration that it *was* a Leonard) is easily worth a thousand. There was still hope, though. Judging by his pained look when he took out his wallet, the man had no idea what a bargain he was getting.

I intercepted him before he reached the car.

"I'll give you ten for that," I said abruptly.

It was a mistake. Vermonters may be wary, but New Jerseyites are paranoid, and I had awoken all his suspicions.

"Naw, it's for the kid," he said.

"Make that twenty."

By way of answering, he slammed the car door and locked all the buttons. His boy had the rod now. I could see him in the back seat as the car disappeared, whacking the tip section over his sisters' heads.

11

August Twenty-third

∞

The river was half its May width. What had been an even, bank-to-bank current was now broken up into separate flows, with scattered rapids that were as small and dainty as the waterfalls in Japanese gardens. Two feet of water had been sliced off the river's top, exposing a lumpy cross-section of boulders and rocks. Places that were chest-deep in June were now only knee-deep, and there were shoal areas to the outside of the pools where the water barely wet my toes.

After all the fitful striving of early season, the river seemed settled and at rest. The heavy current that had hidden so much of its life was gone, and the shallows that were left were as interesting as tidal pools on a saltwater beach. Tiny hellgrammites, graceful water spiders, minnows and miniature trout—they were all there among the rocks, scurrying under the crevices to avoid the monstrous intrusion of my hand.

A day for lazy distraction. A day, that is, for letting life pass dreamily downstream.

I fished in my bathing suit, not my waders—a bathing suit, sneakers and a long-billed swordfisherman's hat that kept the sun from my face. I carried only a few flies: gaudy Royal Coachmans in fan-wing and Wulff ties (against all the rules, but I've found them to be effective low-water patterns), a few Light Cahills and an assortment of terrestri-als. These last are dry flies designed to imitate landbound insects that

tumble into the river. Letort Hoppers, Cinnamon Ants, McMurrays
... There's nothing very complicated about them, ants and grasshoppers not being among your more esoteric insects.

I was using a twenty-year-old fly rod that is already something of a
relic. Back in 1963 when I first started fly fishing, ultralight tackle was
all the rage. Bankrolled by my grandfather's Christmas present, I
ordered Abercrombie and Fitch's "Banty" fly rod—a four-foot bauble
that weighs only an ounce, complete with a special "Banty" fly line
and a Hardy Flyweight reel. I remember my delight when the package
arrived from New York; seconds after opening it, I was false-casting
over the bushes on our snow-covered suburban lawn.

Long graphite rods are the fashion nowadays, and I suppose I elicit
some chuckles when I trot out my "Banty," but the truth is I like it,
and its miniaturization of the whole fishing process suits perfectly my
summertime mood.

I've noticed this before about tackle—how you can fit it to the kind
of attitude you happen to wake up with. On days when I'm feeling
irritated, not to be trifled with, I'm apt to go out with my nine-foot
Browning, a brute of a rod that throws an incredible amount of line
and lets me feel like I'm dominating the river, beating it into
submission. Other days, feeling lazy, I take along an ancient Heddon
that handles an equal amount of line, but is much easier on the arm,
and lets me roll cast without doing much wading. On my last trip to
Britain, I bought a light, seven-foot Hardy; using it, I have to get more
involved with the river, wade more carefully—it's the kind of rod you
feel you should be fishing with on tiptoes, and I save it for my artsier
moods. Those infrequent days when I wake up feeling well-balanced, I
take along my eight-foot Vince Cummings—when it comes to attitude, as neutral a rod as you can find.

The Banty requires a lot of arm work if you're going to get out any
line, and it was half an hour before my casts started unrolling. The
Wulff landed with all the delicacy of an anchor, but the trout must
have been amused by it, and I immediately began to have strikes.
Strikes, not fish. I had assumed the trout would be in a sluggish mood
to match the water, but they all seemed jet-propelled, and the fly was
in and out of their mouths before I could hook them.

Just as catching fish will make a fly fisherman quicker to react, not catching fish dulls his senses, leads him into temptations he would otherwise avoid. I was just above the Aquarium, in the shallow, even stretch before the falls. There's lots of shade here, and the trout will drop back from the sunny stretch above it to cool off. With the reduced current, drag was less of a problem than in spring, and I was getting rises on some very long drifts.

I let the fly drop near some overhanging shrubbery near the bank, and was stripping in line when I noticed something drifting toward me about six inches below the surface. It was a rose—a red rose broken off at its stem, floating perfectly upright downstream, as magically as in a fairy tale.

It was as nice a conflict as a person could be offered, but a conflict all the same. What should I do? Reach down and pluck the rose from the water before it vanished downstream, or continue stripping in the line, thereby being ready for a strike?

My bride of three weeks liked roses. I dropped my left hand from the line and stuck it underwater to intercept the flower; at the same moment, not ten feet away, a fish clobbered my drifting fly. I struck back at him, but he was already gone, and in my haste I dropped the rose and it vanished downstream over the falls.

No fish. No rose. There was a message there somewhere, but I'll be damned if I could figure out what it was. It seemed like a good time to break for lunch.

There was a sandbar along the opposite bank. After finishing my sandwich, I stretched out in the shade with my eyes closed, enjoying the sounds and smells of the summer day. These seemed to come in pairs. There was the rich, heavy smell of newly cut hay with the clanking sound of a tractor; the steady buzz of insects with the sweet aroma of honeysuckle.

I may have dozed for a while. When I woke up, it was to the voices of two young boys engaged in a furious argument. Shading my eyes in the glare, I made them out a hundred yards upstream, bumping down the river in inner tubes.

I say bumping, because that's exactly what they were doing. There wasn't enough water to float the tubes. They would get a little headway in the rapids above the pools, then come to an ignominious stop on the rocks below. Stranded, they stood up in the center of the tubes and waddled over to the bank, yelling at each other all the while.

One of them was bleeding from a cut on his knee; the other's bathing suit was ripped along the side. They acted glad to see an adult.

"We're floating the river in inner tubes," the redheaded one said.

"So I see."

"There's not enough water," his friend added.

"We should have gone last week like I said!" redhead yelled.

"Come off of it!"

"You come off of it!"

It seemed like a good time to intervene.

"Those are pretty unusual tubes," I said. "What's this for over here?"

They had customized them, adding extra strips of rubber to act as bumpers, lashing orange bike pennants to the sides so they could find each other if they became separated. An extra tube had been attached to the redhead's for supplies, but it had hit a sharp rock and sunk. They had started up by the North Branch at 8:30 in the morning, and at this rate, they figured they'd make it to the Connecticut in October.

I helped them relaunch their tubes.

"Watch out for the dam," I said, pushing them out.

They looked at each other. "Uh, what dam?" redhead said.

I told them. They didn't seem impressed.

"No sweat!"

They were bouncing down through the Aquarium now, spinning around as if on snow saucers, and in between their continued arguing, I heard their whoops of joy.

They took a lot of life with them when they left. It was midafternoon, and the hazy sun was pressing down with all its weight. The farmer had left off haying—even the insects seemed muzzled. I tried a few casts, but it was too hot to fish. My rod hidden in the grass, I was getting ready to dive in for a swim when my second visitor of the afternoon arrived: a solitary duck the like of which I had never seen.

He came floating down the river as awkwardly as the boys. I think he was a mallard, though I'm not sure; he had a mallard's neck, but his feathers were as multicolored and scruffy as a Manhattan pigeon's, and he swam with the grace of a turkey.

We immediately became friends. I'm a sucker for open personalities, and this was a duck that held nothing back. He swam right up to me looking for a handout, and when he saw I had nothing for him, decided to stick with me anyhow. I was wading downstream toward a deeper swimming hole, and he tagged along at my heels.

All was fine for the first ten yards, then he fell behind. The low water confused him. He managed all right in depths over eight inches, but when it got shallower than that, he would bump into partly submerged rocks and be unsure whether to swim over them or climb them—at every rock his webbed feet slithered back and forth in indecision. He was embarrassed—he kept rearing back in his best threat posture, his wings beating furiously as he tried to bluff each boulder from his path.

He kept me company while I swam. Occasionally, he would wander off a bit, duck his head underwater and come up with weeds. He worked these furiously through his beak, then spit them out with distaste, like a kid eating spinach. Was he fishing? I was trying to remember if ducks ate fish, when with a quickness I wouldn't have credited him with, he ducked his head again and came up with a minnow.

I never saw anyone take a fish with such commotion and pride. Fish was wiggling around in its beak, duck was going through contortions to keep him there; fish was limp, duck was struggling to climb up onto the bank with him; fish was swallowed, duck was stretching his wings in the threat posture again, quacking in triumph.

"Way to go, duck," I said, saluting him.

Praise is what that duck was after all along. Getting it, he headed downstream in the same direction as the rose and the boys and the day, bumping from rock to rock like a pinball, battered but proud.

12

Really Good Stuff

∞

T he good stuff—the really good stuff—is in the back beneath the
grinning fox. The rest of the store has at least five incarnations.
Go in the door on the right and it's a typical Vermont gift shop, with
maple fudge, wooden tomahawks and postcards. Go in the middle
door, the one that sets the bell jangling, and it's a typical Vermont
drugstore, with liniments for aching muscles, syrups for scratchy
throats and balms for softening the udders of cows.

It's at the edges of Sanborn's where things start to get interesting.
You're out of the new part of the store now (new as in 1870
something), into the older wing where the floorboards sag beneath
your feet and you have to duck to get out of the way of the antique
clothing—the flapper dresses, capes and evening gowns—that hang
suspended from the ceiling, their sleeves wafting gently as if swayed by
invisible arms.

The wine is there to the right on three long shelves. It's a democratic
assemblage, amusing in its lack of pretension, but with a . . . how shall
we say it? . . . *mongrel* breeding: a few Moselles for class, a token
Liebfraumilch, a cloudy looking White Mountain white, maple wine
bottled in Vermont, a few of the pop Italian brands and whatever other
curiosities Mr. Sanborn happens to enjoy. You can either spring for a
bottle now and take a chance you'll have enough for flies, or wait until
you buy the flies and get the cheaper vintage with what's left.

A ramp leads to the back. The battered thirty-five–cent paperbacks are on either side; browsing through them is like leafing through the best-seller lists of the last thirty years. *A Generation of Vipers, Travels with Charley, Advise and Consent, Anatomy of a Murder, Growing Up Absurd, Peyton Place, The Godfather, Jaws.* Past them, the real bookshelves begin, with over a thousand old volumes. The section on Vermont is beneath the moosehead, the one that drools papier-mâché; included are *27th Vermont Agricultural Report 1907, University of Vermont Service Records 1917–18, History of Athens, VT, Ancient Craft Masonry in Vermont, The Autobiography of Calvin Coolidge,* and—even better—*Grace Coolidge and Her Era.*

If you follow the town histories down into Massachusetts, then cross over to the shelf on war books, then follow the fiction past the cookbooks, you're into good stuff, but not the really good stuff: spinning rods hanging from their tips, bait buckets stacked haphazardly in the corner, lures taped by cellophane to the walls. These are bass lures; is there anything more typically American in proud illiteracy and cartoon rhythm than their names? River Runt, Bugeye, Cop-e-cat, Flutterchuck, Hawg Frawg, Krocodile, Lusox, Sputterbug, Kweet Special, Auger-tail, Bopper Popper . . . they're all here, with a flash and energy that are as aural as sound.

Between the bass lures and the really good stuff is a wood stove, a big Defiant. It's seldom on. Propped against its cold side are some old paintings, the kind that itinerant artists would toss off in the 1850s, workmanlike imitations of the Hudson River school, landscapes featuring valleys, castles and clouds. Never mind their holes. For ten dollars, they're atmospheric bargains to hang on old walls.

You're in the remotest corner of the store now, into the really good stuff at last—the flies, nets, fly rods and reels. The stuffed fox hangs from the ceiling over the fly-tying supplies; he's mounted with one paw lifted in a pose that manages to be bloodthirsty and delicate at the same time, and as you browse through the fly trays, you wonder whether he's snarling at you or smiling.

Ah, the fly trays. They're a glorious mess. The Bivisibles are mixed in with the streamers, the terrestrials are combined with the nymphs, and the midges are God knows where. It takes a good half hour to find what you're looking for. At the bottom of one tray is a snelled bass fly with a huge yellow wing, the kind Doctor Henshall might have used; at the bottom of another is a Parmacheene Belle, or some other antique.

About the time you make your selection, Mr. Sanborn will appear. He looks like a moody Santa Claus, with a belly that spills over his belt, a snow-white beard and an introspective frown. He's wearing wool pants and a checkered shirt—it makes him look like Santa all right, but a Santa who runs a trap line on the side.

"Help you there?"

Unless you're a local, Mr. Sanborn won't recognize you, no matter how many times you've been in his store. He'll recommend some flies, then fill you in on his fishing. This won't be on the river (he last fished it in the 1940s, and according to him it's been going downhill ever since), but on the nearby lakes. Downriggers with Golden Demons in ten feet of water, he says. Ten trout last night, twelve the night before.

"You fish them like I tell you, see what happens. Jigger it right back to you soon as they bite. Ayuh, that's fishing."

His voice is deep, comforting. You can dig away at the flies while he talks. You can wonder whether the fox is happy or sad, puzzle out what kind of wine you should buy, and make a mental note to find out, someday, exactly what *Grace Coolidge and Her Era* is all about.

I'm lucky to have Sanborn's so close. A good tackle shop can complement a good river, act as prelude to its delights. Ordering tackle through the mail is a sterile pleasure in comparison; what the fly fisherman needs are fly trays to paw through, reels to click experimentally, rods to wiggle appraisingly in his hand. Just as the rivers I've fished seem to link themselves in my memory into one long river, the tackle shops I've known seem to merge into one gigantic store, a cornucopia of impressions departmentalized by the years.

Bob's Bait comes first, fragrant with the smell of coffee-ground-bedded worms. It wasn't far from the lake where I learned to fish, and we would stop there for shiners on our way to the boat. As tackle shops go, it was small—maybe ten by five at the most. Roughly two-thirds of that space was taken up by galvanized tanks for the bait; into the rest was crammed an incredible assortment of rods, reels and lures. An acquisitive twelve, I couldn't go into the store without drooling—I never wanted anything as much as I did those cleverly displayed lures.

Bob himself was an impassive man with a martyred expression; whenever I tried to tell him about the fish I had caught on his bait, he grunted and turned away, leaving me close to tears. I couldn't imagine anyone selling such marvelous stuff being less than marvelous himself, and it was a great disappointment to learn that Bob was totally pedestrian, with very little interest in fishing, and even less interest in humoring enthusiastic boys. Looking back, I suppose his feet hurt or something—that's the only expression I ever saw on his face.

I had been buying lures at Bob's with increasing reluctance when a competitor opened up closer to town. The Angler's Pool was everything Bob's Bait was not, with immaculate display cases trimmed with cherry, fly tackle arranged in spacious rows and a friendly and knowledgeable owner. Franz had come originally from Germany, and his accent added just the right amount of exoticism to his gear. He loved to talk fishing. I would show up in the morning when no customers were around (I found out later that no customers were *ever* around), and he would take me out back to his stockroom to show me the latest order that had come in.

Poor Franz! He was a collector, not a shopkeeper, and his love for fine tackle soon did him in. Fly fishermen with the money for good equipment were scarce in that town; by the end of the summer, he was out of business—the shop was turned into a beautician's. As a parting gift, Franz gave me a dozen of his best Light Cahills.

Bob, of course, continued to prosper, scowl and all. It was an early lesson in economics: when it came to tackle shops, good guys, or at least good fly-fishermen, did not finish first.

The Angler's Pool had initiated me into the pleasures of classy tackle shops. Casting about for a replacement, I went right to the source: Abercrombie and Fitch.

Poor A & F! Like Franz's, its New York store was having trouble staying in business, faced as it was with competition from the cut-rate sporting goods stores like Herman's, and the mail-order houses like

Bean's. The outdoors was being democratized in the '60s, and Abercrombie and Fitch's eliteness seemed too fuddy-duddy to endure. I suppose the market for $200 croquet sets and elephant-hide footrests was never a very big one to begin with, even at the best of times.

Though its glories were fading when I knew it, there was still enough glitter left to impress a fourteen-year-old boy. I would take the train into the city, walk crosstown from Penn Station to Madison Avenue. There were bookstores along the way, record stores, too, but I sailed past them like Ulysses past the Sirens, saving my three or four dollars of spending money until I got to Abercrombie and Fitch itself.

It always seemed to be raining when I got there; the store was in its autumnal phase, and everything in it had a patina of venerability and age. Walking through the door into the ground-level floor was like walking into the British Museum—the accessories displayed there seemed the spoils of Empire—and it was hard to remember that everything was for sale. You never noticed the cash registers. Were they even there?

I took the elevator right to the fishing tackle on the eighth floor. They were great elevators. They'd be filled with stuffy-looking businessmen on their lunch hours; I loved their baldness, their quaint tweed, the authoritative way they reached out and pushed the button on the floor of their choice.

I stepped out onto the eighth floor with the excitement with which other kids must have entered Disneyland. There was some really good stuff there! Over in the left-hand corner by the elevator bank was a gold-plated fighting chair, the kind Hemingway must have used for marlin, and jutting out from it was a tuna rod with two tips—*two* tips, branching apart from the butt to form a Y. To the right of it, the fly tackle began—I remember how beautifully brown the bamboo rods were, how afraid I was to touch them. The flies were in long flat wooden trays, displayed as delicately as butterflies. Beyond them were the bass lures, at double the price of Bob's. Along the wall were glass display cases with the reels—I remember a miniature bait-casting reel that shone in the fluorescent light like an emerald. Scattered about the counter's top were Wheatley fly boxes and streamer wallets lined with wool. Further to the right was a bookcase, with books by people like Edward R. Hewitt and George M. L. LaBranche, authors whose ghosts probably still shopped there once the regular customers were gone.

All of the sales clerks looked like Herbert Hoover. I don't think any of them ever deigned to wait on me. They acted like they worked there merely as a genteel means of killing time between fishing trips—asking one of them for help was like breaking the silence in the reading room of Mycroft Holmes's private club.

I never dared do that. I would walk around for a while trying to find something my three dollars would buy, then—since the A & F elevators seemed only to ascend and never descend—sadly take the stairs down to the street. Three dollars went a long way in those days, but only at Nedick's.

I shouldn't have laughed at the sales clerks. Before long, I was working as one myself—at Macy's, the biggest store in the world. It was 1969. I was dropping out of college with a certain degree of regularity, trying to find the time to write. Macy's seemed like a reasonable stopgap. In those days, the shoe clerks all wanted to be tap dancers, the lingerie women dreamed of being Carol Channing, and the luggage department had more poets than Columbia.

They put me in sporting goods; as far as I know, I was the first would-be novelist they'd had. The rest of the group was varied enough. Gus the Greek was thirty-four and aggressively single; he was a storehouse of information on singles bars, '50s rock singers and bluefishing. Tom O'Brien was a former All-Ireland drum major who had brought his strut with him to America; it was hard to know where the blarney left off and the truth began—he was too small to have played international rugby for Ireland, but you had to listen to his stories or he'd get mad. Jim was a recently returned Vietnam veteran —none of us probed his silences too hard. Bob Stern, our boss, was smooth-talking and ambitious, but took a boyish delight in breaking store rules, and was something of a hero to us for that reason.

In those days, sporting goods was in what was called the ''Outdoor

Shop.'' It was a separate wing from the main store, and the floorwalkers pretty much left us alone. The rest of the clerks got twenty minutes for their breaks—we all took forty. Our lunch hours were apt to start around eleven and end shortly before three. Times when business was slow, we'd go down to the stock room and start up games of whiffle ball or hockey; Gus once broke a window with a slap shot and set off all the alarms.

I was the resident intellectual. Bob Stern would keep me busy forging letters from customers to Macy's president raving about how courteous and helpful the clerks in sporting goods were; Tom O'Brien had me draft letters to Queen Elizabeth denouncing British policy in Ulster. I was paid for these in fishing tackle.

It worked this way. Management was always putting pressure on Stern to get rid of his unsold inventory by putting it on sale. These were unadvertised sales; he'd mark things down and put them out on a table. It soon occurred to us that no one at Macy's cared how little these items sold for—the important thing was to get rid of them. We all had our favorite sport. What we started to do was deliberately order things we wanted, hold them for a while in the stock room, then without telling anyone, put them up for sale at outrageous prices and buy them ourselves.

There were some great bargains. Gus got a brand-new AMF bowling ball for eighty-five cents; Jim got a Shakespeare hunting bow for a quarter. Our consciences didn't bother us very much; after all, these sales were available to the public, too—available, that is, if they could get into the store before the 10 o'clock opening.

I did quite well for myself. There was an Italian spinning reel marked down from $59.99 to ninety-nine cents; a Garcia fly rod that went for a quarter; Cortland fly lines for ten cents; Rapala plugs at five for a nickel. By the time Stern got transferred and the scam came to an end, I had enough fishing tackle to last the next twenty years.

In a way, the cheap gear at Macy's was too much of a good thing. It ruined tackle shops for me, at least temporarily. Having bought so much for so little, I couldn't bear paying full retail for a rod or reel.

There were other tackle shops in the next few years, but none with sufficient charisma to recreate that former allure.

It was 1976 before I found another one worthy enough to add to my collection. I was spending the autumn in London, and on rainy afternoons would take the tube to St. James Park and cross over to Hardy's on Pall Mall.

Hardy's, of course, was the snobbiest fishing store in the world. When it came to disdain, the clerks made Abercrombie and Fitch's look like Kiwanians. This gave them a certain historical charm—with all the changes in the world, it was nice to find a place where you could still be patronized as a rude colonial. For a long time, I was tempted to buy one of their Northumbrian jackets. It's a waxed game coat, the kind you can't buy in the States, but at sixty pounds it was too far out of reach. Still, I enjoyed trying them on. A clerk gave me his understated sales pitch the first time, but after that they began to recognize me, and I was left to browse in peace.

British tackle shops are five or six times more interesting than American ones. They understand about shops in Britain—there are no malls, and the people that wait on you have a broad knowledge of their sport. Hardy's aside, I've found them quick to ask about American fishing, and generous in their advice. I visited two tiny shops in Chester last year. One was devoted to fly fishing, one to coarse fishing. In the first, I had a delightful conversation with the owner about trout; in the second, I listened for an hour to a monologue on roach. It was a fine afternoon.

Now when I go to Europe I make it a habit to stop at any tackle shop I can find. You get a lot of instant camaraderie that way; you can also find some really good stuff. The best souvenir I've ever bought came from a small tackle shop in Paris on the Seine: a twelve-foot-long metal pole, the kind those eternal Parisian fishermen use on the quays. The best fly boxes I've ever seen come from a shop on the Zentral-strasse in Berne; the Swiss have a way with miniaturization and these boxes are spaciously compact.

It's a long journey from Bob's Bait in Connecticut to Hardy's of Pall Mall. From Hardy's to Sanborn's of Vermont is in a sense an even longer trip, for my attitude toward tackle shops has evolved over the years. I no longer want the predictable rows of mass-produced rods and raygun-looking reels, but shop instead for the unexpected and offbeat. I have a Vermont river that is varied, full of wonder. The shop that goes with it must be the same.

Sanborn's. Liniment, udder softener, antique clothing, wine, books and flies. My kind of store at last.

13

A Home by the River

ᗡᗡᗡ

There's a piece of land for sale on the river, six acres of meadow, pine and oak rising gently from the south bank. Through the middle runs a stream no bigger than a person's stride, a stream bridged by weathered planks that creak as they sag. An old woods road runs up to the open field at the hill's crest. There are wild blackberries growing along the edges of this road, blueberries further up in the sun. A spring on top provides water. The view east is of hills and farms and the sunrise.

I walked up to it yesterday in the middle of a summer rain. The small, hand-lettered For Sale sign had been nailed to a tree on the far side of the river since May, and though I had been tempted several times, it was only now that I had gotten around to crossing over.

It's good land. If you poke around abandoned hill farms as much as I do, you come to have a sense of whether the land you're walking on was once cherished or once cursed. Shadows that never disappear, even in winter; ground that is rockier than most Vermont ground; stone walls that seem hastily thrown together, as if hurled there by the farmer in his frustration at tilling such soil ... these are all tokens of land that has been detested, to be avoided no matter how cheaply it may be had. No sunlight for those solar panels you plan so hopefully to install; no soil for the tomatoes your wife wants to plant; a well that dries up every June—land that broke people in the 1780s can break

people in the 1980s, in subtle, persistent ways.

My parcel (and how ready I was to call it mine!) had traces of a gentle hand. Someone had taken pains in cutting the road, looping it in gradual curves that understood the contours of the hill. In clearing the meadow, they had spared many of the trees—some of the oaks I was walking under were probably as old as any in Vermont. The stone wall that ran along the western boundary was skillfully arranged, not merely dumped; someone had matched flat rock to flat rock, round one to round one, and it was a masterpiece of its kind. The land, having once been loved, could be loved again.

I found a stump to sit on under a hemlock that held back some of the rain. Our house, I quickly decided, should go in the center of the meadow facing the river. The oaks would provide shade in the summer, but by fall their leaves would be gone and there would be sunlight to warm the bay window in our study. I could write there. We could have a library on the side, with built-in shelves for our books, cedar cabinets for our rods. The bedroom would be upstairs where the last sound we'd hear at night would be the voice of the river. A guest room would go nicely above the garage. A guest room with a large picture window facing east so all our friends could enjoy the view we had come to love.

There would be fishing, of course—fishing that required no advance planning or long drive, but came as easily as a whim on a warm summer's night. The water there is not the best trout water on the river, but its broad and easy air would wear well over the years. There are no deep pools or fast runs. You get the feeling there are only small trout there, not monsters, and it frees you from the burden of catching them. It would be a fine stretch of river on which to teach a child to fish.

I dreamed, in short, of a home that would be worthy of the river that ran by it. There are dozens of homes in this valley; many are weathered farmhouses that blend into their setting as only New England homes can, yet they all turn their backs on the river, and not a single one has been built deliberately to enjoy it.

Wondering about this, I began thinking not only of the land I was walking on and the home my dreams erected, but of the valley and its future. Was it wrong in the 1980s to put all your love into a piece of unspoiled earth? Wrong to think that the work and worry and hope that went into it would ever be requited by anything except pollution and development and noise? More to the point: did anyone cherish this river besides me? Even to pose the question like that was an egotistical conceit, but I was considering the river's future now, adding up its allies, and it was a question worth asking.

The farmers cherish it in their sober, undemonstrative way. I hear them speak sadly whenever a good piece of farmland is gone back to trees or sold to summer people, and the river is why their own land continues productive when all the hill farms have been abandoned. You can catch them staring off toward it in their rare respites from work; after a lifetime of toil, it must come to seem a brotherly presence in the year's slow turn.

Anyone else beside them? Do the fishermen who come here cherish it? I don't think so, not as they should. The people from town fish it in spring and at no other time, and I've followed enough of them through the pools to know they are the ones dumping bottles and cans. The fly fishermen I meet are almost inevitably out-of-staters, and though they may value the river for its productivity, their interest is of necessity only brief and intermittent.

The river is not famous. There are no summer resorts along its banks, no major ski areas or tourist attractions. Sometimes I think that it is this very obscurity that saves the river, makes it worth loving. Other times, I know I'm wrong, realize that the only thing that will save the valley from the development that will one day come isn't neglect, but the concerted efforts of people who love it as I do, people whom I fear are simply not there. Conservationists have banded together to save portions of the Beaverkill and the wild sections of the St. John, but what of all the smaller, more obscure rivers in between? How many of these vanish with hardly a whimper, undefended and unloved?

Vermonters are easy marks for developers. Their insistence on being able to do what they please with their land makes them reject zoning out-of-hand; their distrust of anything abstract makes them suspicous

of regional planning and imposed controls. Times are bad here now—
there are people in this valley who live in cold trailers throughout the
winter. In the face of their poverty, meeting their eyes, it would be
hard to argue against the construction of a new highway or large
factory, yet either would doom them just as surely as it would doom
the river. Development brings in skilled workers from Massachusetts
with whom they can't compete; better highways bring in commuters
with money, drive up the land to prices young families can't afford.

The trend has already started. The six acres I was walking across
would have sold for two or three thousand dollars as recently as five
years ago, but with the condos and second homes inching closer, it was
probably priced at eleven thousand or twelve. I wondered if we could
afford that with a house. I began to think of mortgage payments,
insurance, building permits, taxes. I thought of those things, then I
thought of the income the kind of fiction worth writing brings in. My
dream house, so easily created, just as easily disappeared.

If it weren't for reality, none of us would have any problems. Still, it
costs nothing to dream, and it's a time-honored way of spending a
rainy afternoon. I walked slowly back down the road from the
meadow, doing my best to rid my thoughts of the future and
concentrate on the here and now. The rain, so gentle at first, had
changed just as gradually as my mood, and fell now with a cool and
determined hardness, rattling the trees as loudly as hail.

The wind, switching directions, blew from the north. There was the
smell of damply packed earth, the sound of a distant chain saw. A leaf
fell ahead of me on the road, then a second, then a third, and as easily
and gracefully as that it was fall.

In a hurry now, I turned my collar against the rain and climbed
down through another man's land to my car.

14

A Year of September

○○○

The best day of the year to go fishing is the first day of school. Leaving early, you drive past children waiting by the road for the bus—newly clothed, sneakers white, immaculate; skin scrubbed as shiny as pot bottoms, hair glossy as palominos', obediently banged, ponytailed, shagged, whatevered; book bags slack, empty, like deflated balloons; pencils stiletto sharpened, pens bursting blue; voices raised, biceps pinched, races run, footballs tossed; children, that is, with their lightly worn burden of crabby teacher, bossy coach, unrepentant bully, unrequited love, pickled beets, algebra, condemned to spend this fairest of September days locked indoors, regretting summer, hatching plots, humming revolutionary song ("Mine eyes have seen the glory of the burning of the school"), wishing more than anything to be outside. You pass all these, and you head on toward the river to play with trout, unscrubbed, unshaven, nonimmaculate but *free*.

In the valleys that run west from the Connecticut, there is a direct correlation between wealth and no trespassing signs. In the more affluent valleys they are everywhere, so thick it makes it seem as if the owners of the land are trying to lock the rivers away in boxes, each slat of which is another sign: VIOLATORS WILL BE PROSECUTED TO THE FULL EXTENT OF THE LAW!

Travel up to the poorer valleys that begin north of the White River

107

and you will see few such signs. The Vermonters who live there are still too close to the old days to make much sense out of the kind of miserliness that puts limits on the land's enjoyment. On the river, I can think of only one no trespassing sign, but it's in a vital spot, and it involved me in three seconds of moral dilemma.

Below the elementary school is a powerful chute I had never fished before. On my third cast with a yellow Marabou, I hooked a rainbow who immediately tore off downstream, right through the middle of a deep pool.

I couldn't coax him back in the current, nor could I follow him downstream through the pool—it was well over my head. My only recourse was to take to shore and follow him along the bank. I had started . . . I had gone about five yards . . . when I ran smack into a big NO TRESPASSING sign and a rusty strand of barbed wire.

I hesitated, both because I was surprised, and because that black print was so intimidating. No Experience Allowed This Side of Me, the sign seemed to say—No Enjoyment, No Wonder, No Curiosity, No Joy. I thought about it for a second, then I thought about Woody Guthrie's "This Land is Your Land, This Land is My Land," and the last verse, the one they don't sing in the easy-listening versions or teach the kids in school.

> As I was walking that dusty highway,
> I saw a sign said Private Property,
> But on the other side, the sign said nothing,
> That side was made for you and me!

And stepping over that barbed wire, I went in pursuit of my trout.

The leaves have been slow to turn this year. I drove to the river on the 10th expecting to see those early reds and yellows that lead the way into autumn, but everything remained stubbornly green. The only colors I found were on dead maple leaves lying along the banks. There was a yellowish-red flush to their scalloped edges, a deeper red where the veins came together near the stem.

Where had they come from? Further upstream where it was higher and wilder, solidly fall? Spontaneously generated from the crispness in the air? There weren't any bare trees around and their presence was mystifying. They seemed plotted—arranged. They overlay each other on the rocks like decoys set in sunshine to lure the other leaves down.

September means morning fog in Vermont. If you were flying in a glider across the mountains you could look down and see tributary fog in narrow white seams, each of which hides a valley. The seams gain amplitude as they flow east, joining snowier bands, merging finally with the great fog river that is the Connecticut.

These rivers are lifeless from the air, but were your vision somehow to penetrate the white, you might see a fly fisherman at the very bottom—a giant fisherman, his size exaggerated by the magnifying quality fog has. He's casting slowly, blowing on his hands to keep them warm. In summer, the fog hides the sun's heat and is welcomed; in fall, the fog hides the sun's heat and is endured.

Fog is expectation. Something momentous is going to be revealed— you feel it the moment you enter the river. It adds an intenseness to the fishing that can seem almost unbearable. You are in the midst of a secret, *part* of that secret, unable to decipher it from the center. Fog will halo a man, throw a penumbra round his shoulders, but it's a shining that can only be detected from outside.

Morning fog. When it lifted this morning, the sun streamed in on my back like a jet of hot air. Turning, I saw a huge rock that was the last bit of river the fog hid, a glacial wanderer that had come to a stop in the middle of a broad pool. It gradually emerged—the broad tawny base, the narrowing, prow-shaped middle, and then on the very top, the secret. A blue heron, as immobile as the rock itself, watching me with a knowing and patience that were prehistoric, sculpted of the same timelessness as the fog.

There are trade-offs to be made in fishing a river. One may be full of huge trout, but be impossible to wade; another is wadeable, but too crowded to enjoy. Each trout stream carries with it these contradictions, and it's up to the fisherman to reconcile them as best he can.

Take my river, for instance. The wading is a pleasure—the bottom is firm and comfortably rocky, and there's enough room so the trees don't imperil your casts. The valley is beautiful, fishing pressure is light and trout are abundant in three varieties. Big trout, however, are scarce. The three- and four-pounders are down in the White River or over in the Lamoille, and to take anything over fourteen inches is cause for celebration.

All the more reason, then, to rue the trout I missed yesterday morning. I was chest-deep in the Aquarium, casting upstream with a grasshopper imitation. Earlier in the season I couldn't have stood there without being tumbled over by the current, but the pressure had eased with autumn and my stance was secure. I had missed a teasing rise over on the left bank; there's a rock a yard out and a trout lying behind it can get first crack at anything drifting over the falls.

I cast again, this time aiming it so the line draped itself over the rock. It's a trick that's worked before; when the line tightens and pulls the fly onto the eddy below the rock you get a vital second of drag-free drift.

Perfect. The grasshopper, landing on the rock, crawled over its downstream edge and hopped into the water. Immediately, a trout was on it—the river fell away as if in the vacuum of a depth charge, and in the gap where water had been appeared a monstrous back. I struck as hard as I could, but tightened on nothing—the fish and its promise were already irretrievable, a moment in the past.

Stripping the line in, I examined my fly. The hook was intact and sharp, but its hackles were flattened, as if it had been scared out if its wits by the trout's ferocity.

A big one, then—a once-in-a-season trout. In missing him, I felt like I had missed some connection with the river itself—had lost a chance to learn something important about its capacities, and the huge swirl with the question mark in the middle tormented me the rest of the day.

I went up to Maurice Page's this afternoon. His shop is on the North Branch, a hundred yards above its confluence with the main river. It's a rickety affair of red boards that contract and expand with the seasons. In the warm September sunshine, the cracks in the walls were fully open, as if the entire shop were inhaling one last time before winter.

COOPER, the sign near the loading platform reads. Above it is another sign, this one hand-lettered: "If I'm not here, honk three times. If I'm still not here, honk some more." Beyond it is a notice warning people that they enter the shop at their own risk. In order to read the faded print you have to enter the shop anyway, so it seems stupid to leave.

There was a big wooden tub on the platform, the kind farmers use to water their cows. Next to it were some boards that Maurice hadn't gotten around to cutting. Closer to the edge were footstools, birdhouses and printer's trays, the kind of things Maurice keeps in sight in case any stray tourists happen by.

An important October birthday was coming up, and I had my eye on one of his chests. Maurice sells them unpainted, for a fair price. Even better, a portion of his personality comes with them, and a blanket chest made by Maurice Page is a lively, solid thing, part of a Vermont that is vanishing.

I was looking one over when Maurice came out. "You don't want it," he said, shaking his head. He opened the lid, then banged it in disgust. "See there? Top don't fit. I messed that one. I've got something better inside. Watch your step now."

Pine is everywhere in the shop—in the corners, on the lathes, in the air. Sawdust and shavings are September smells, sweeter than incense, more honest than perfume, and every leathery inch of Maurice comes bathed in its glow.

"There's your chest," he said, slapping its side. "Course you want, I could make it bigger. Here, come up here."

Deeper and deeper, up the stairs. There's the old water-power transformer near the top, dusty now that the dam is gone (1924 was the date it went out, but Maurice talks about the catastrophe as if it happened yesterday). Among the scraps and leftovers in the loft is a pine board that measures fourteen inches across, and Maurice decides it is just what I need for my chest. We agree on the dimensions—

Maurice hands me the tape measure and lets me do most of the measuring myself.

Maurice is a Vermonter who likes to talk. It's next to impossible to describe the texture of it; in it are weaved strands of laconic understatement, subtle teasing, old-fashioned courtliness, rhetorical interrogation, free association and whatever elocutionary devices Maurice happens to be in the mood for. As he talks, the light from the windows catches the stubble of his beard with the effect of a thousand sequins, making him twinkle.

"Yep, lived here all my life up to now," he'll say if you're a stranger. "Born in that house right there across the road seventy-five years ago." Then, if you're a woman: "You come up here in winter, I'll take you for a ride in my snow machine, don't forget now."

We talked for a while. A documentary had recently been made of another cooper up in Barnet, and I asked Maurice if he had seen it.

"Wasn't that a marvel? That Ben, he's a wizard. Aren't too many of those fellas left still use water power. Me, I flick a switch, on it goes."

He reached behind him. Instantly, the pulleys, gears and belts that line his shop clanked into action. He waited until the shop was really shaking, then shut it off.

"Nope, don't pay me now," he said when he saw my wallet. "I might not finish it, and then what happens? I don't want to be in debt to you, do I?"

We settled upon a pick-up date. I turned the car around in the cutoff and was circling past the shop when he flagged me down.

"Here's a wooden spoon," he said, jabbing it in the open window. "Good for porridge. Give it to your mom."

There's a short story by V. S. Pritchett about a businessman who's good at falling down. Whenever he's at a loss for words, bored, embarrassed or surprised, down he goes. It's his only talent. He knows a dozen ways to do it; when the story ends, he's showing off his latest tumble to his aghast business associates at an important meeting.

It's a character I can relate to. I've had some classic falls of my own this month, half of them caused by impatience, half by my dislike for waders. I've been fishing in jeans and sneakers since summer, and the cold water has finally caught up with me. I clanked from pool to pool like a wind-up monster with rusty gears, an angling Frankenstein.

There's a good lie near the cemetery that can only be covered by casting from a rock in midstream. I was halfway up it when I slipped. As falls go, it was only fair—say an 8.5 in difficulty, a 7.5 in execution. Still, it was enough to drench me and I had to hurry back to the car for a dry set of clothes.

My waders are the cheapest kind you can get, slippery, ill-fitting and porous. Wading wet, though, was out of the question, so I tugged them on. What I gained in warmth, I lost in traction, and later in the afternoon I took another spill, this one much more spectacular than the first.

I was back in the Aquarium, stalking the big trout I had missed earlier in the month. We'd had the usual heavy rain around the equinox, and the water was higher than it had been the previous time—high enough to increase the force on my legs and feet. About a foot to my left was a nice flat boulder that would allow me to get above the worst of the pressure. I shuffled over to it and gingerly stepped onto its middle.

False-casting about twenty yards of line out, I dropped a big Spuddler a foot above the rock where the trout had struck. As the fly landed, I shifted position slightly, just enough so that the tread under my weight-bearing foot slid from the security of gritty granite to the peril of slippery moss.

It was a backwards somersault this time, a fall I had never pulled off before, not even in school. What was remarkable about it was its slow-motion quality—I had enough time and horizon left at the apogee to see a huge boil beneath the fly. Upside down, I yanked back with my rod hand, but there was no rod there—it was flying through the air behind me with the arc and thrust of a javelin.

"I must prepare myself for this," I thought, but before I could, I was splashing in the water, already past the icy shock of entry. I grabbed for my sunglasses, but the current had them on the bottom, scurrying over the rocks like a plastic crab. I started to chase after them, but the river was in my waders, and the weight tumbled me over so that I was floating face-up. My wallet, buoyed free of my pocket, bubbled dollar bills past my chest; my fly box, sprung from my vest, bobbed like the coffin of the *Pequod*.

There was no use fighting it. I gave myself up to my klutziness and let the current push me over to a sandbar—a lump now, a sack of wet nothingness to be stripped clean and flung disdainfully on the shore. Somewhere in my passage from vertical to horizontal to vertical again I managed to bump heads with a rock, resulting in a concussion that laid me up for three days, giving me plenty of time to puzzle out the moral of all this.

Never underestimate the capacity of a river to humiliate you, and always wear felt-bottomed soles.

Autumn is leaf-peeping time in Vermont, and after a few sudden stops you learn not to tailgate out-of-state cars. Of all the unofficial seasons here (mud season and black-fly season are the two others), foliage season is by far the silliest. While flatlanders are peeping at the leaves, natives are peeping at the peepers, and peeping-atrocity stories are numerous.

I have two this year. I was driving over a hill on I-91 this morning when I came upon a station wagon with New York plates parked right in the middle of the northbound lane—*in* the lane, not on its edge. A man in a safari suit was sitting on the opened tailgate studying the view with his binoculars; a willowy blonde sat on the hood absorbed in a sketchbook. I honked at them—they waved pleasantly as I swerved past.

The second happened on the river. I was on my knees trying to revive a small brookie before letting him go when I heard someone beeping a horn up by my car. Tourists had been stopping all morning to take pictures of me against the trees, and I assumed it was someone wanting me to pose. I swam the trout back and forth until he was able to manage on his own, then waded over to the road.

Ohio plates, a carful of peepers. The man who was driving stuck his head out the window—it had a red and mushy look, like stewed tomatoes.

"Where's this desert thing at?" he demanded.

I have this strange capacity to understand illogical questions. Most people would have looked at the man in incomprehension; I understood right away which desert he was after.

"You mean the Desert of Maine?" I said, referring to a popular tourist spot.

"Yeah, that desert thing, Where's it at, pal?"

"You take this road over to New Hampshire, then turn left on Route 10 up to 302. It's right down that about 180 miles."

"Thanks, pal."

Off they went.

And just for the record, the foliage peaked this year at precisely 3:38 P.M. on Thursday, September 29. I was there when it happened. I was fishing by the elementary school, and had stopped to stare in awe at the trees. There were dark storm clouds overhead, the wind would be stripping most of the leaves off by dusk, but for now the black sky framed perfectly the bittersweet reds and yellows, giving them a color so vibrant and urgent that their radiation was a tug on the heart.

As I watched, something remarkable happened. The sun found a hole in the cloud just large enough for one crepuscular ray to leap through. It slanted obliquely toward earth, catching a gold tree on the bank and casting its radiance onto the surface of the river, spinning it gold. My fly rode on its shimmer for the space of a yard—for that one fleeting moment I was fishing a golden fly for golden trout on a golden river. Then the cloud clamped shut around the sun, and the peak was passed.

I heard voices up on the bank. A boy and girl, each about eight, were kicking through the leaves piled against the trees. Every few yards they stooped to pick one up and put it in a plastic bag they jointly carried.

They waved, and came over to watch me. As it turned out, the leaves were for their oldest sister, in college out west. She was homesick for Vermont's autumn, she had written; they were collecting a bagful of the yellowest yellows and the reddest reds to send her to cheer her up.

"Here's one for you," the girl said, handing me a maple leaf.

"Thanks, I'll keep it on my desk this winter. It will remind me of September."

The boy saw his chance.

"September," he said, spreading his arms apart as if to embrace the smells, the colors and light, "is my best favorite year."

15

Fathers and Sons

○○○

Between the years 1961 and 1966, I was the most obnoxious teenager to fish with in all of New England, and if you don't believe me, ask my Dad. Vain, overzealous, opinionated, dictatorial, insufferable, fierce—any combination of negative adjectives would aptly describe the tall redhead I can see in my mind's eye casting from the bow of the battered, fifteen-foot runabout, and it was my poor father, casting patiently from the stern, who took their brunt.

Fishing fathers, fishing sons. The literature on the subject is immense, and invariably follows the same pattern. Wise, experienced, pipe-smoking father (Big Bill) teaches eager, barefooted, gum-chewing son (Little Bill) the tenets of good sportsmanship, the better to tame the youngster's fish-killing propensities. ("It's a noble brown, Little Bill. Let us raise our hats to him and give him his freedom!") Teaching a son to fly fish has become a sacred duty, a rite of passage, a cliché.

And, of course, a very difficult chore. It's not easy to instill tradition in a teenager whose every instinct is to smash tradition. I saw a father and son on the river who perfectly illustrated the problem. Both were dressed in the same wader–fishing-vest–Tyrolian hat combination; both fished with expensive rods. I could see the father teaching the son how to roll cast—the son was nodding, albeit grimly. There were trout rising in the next pool, and the father went to investigate. Left alone, the son started whipping the water in front of him with his rod—

actually whipping it, as if punishing the river for some infraction . . .
No, not an easy chore at all.

In our family, it was backwards. I was the one who taught my father
how to fish, damned near killing him in the process. Naturally, I
harbor a lot of guilt about this. The memory of how I treated him goes
with me each time I fish the river, descending like a sudden black cloud
on an otherwise perfect day. One taste of the madeleine was enough to
recreate for Proust the chaotic emotions of youth, and so it is with me.
One snarled leader, one sloppy cast, and I am fifteen years old again,
slapping the side of our boat in impatience, giving my father hell.

Life puts a statute of limitations on the apologies that are due
between a father and son, a few quick years after which they will
remain permanently unspoken. Here then, before that limit expires, is
mine.

It started the summer I was thirteen. My parents had owned the lake
house for a year, and in that time I had become totally dedicated to
fishing. My long-standing passions for baseball, basketball, cocker
spaniels and West Point were as nothing compared to it; I read every

book on the subject I could get my hands on, subscribed to three different fishing magazines, spent every allowance dollar on lures and flies. It was an enthusiasm with all the force of puberty behind it—whatever I was sublimating, I was sublimating in a big way.

It wasn't long before I considered myself an expert roughly on a par with Lee Wulff. This had nothing to do with catching fish; indeed, it was only about once in every six weeks of casting that I managed to find a trout or bass suicidal enough to take my lure. Teenagers being teenagers, my lack of success only made me more rigid in my theories. I fished where the books said to fish whether I caught anything or not, and sneered at those who caught fish where they weren't supposed to be. In short, I became a fishing snob—a snob who combined an inquisitor's detestation for heresy with a Schweitzer's missionary zeal. Casting about for a disciple to mold in my own image, I found my Dad.

Dad had fished a bit before. Friends from the office would charter a party boat out of Freeport on Long Island and he would go with them, returning at the end of the day heroically sunburnt and unshaved, reeking of flounder. For a time when I was small, we owned a boat of our own with friends of my parents—a leaky wooden cabin cruiser called the *BettyWayna* in honor of the wives. It was over the *BettyWayna*'s side that I caught my first fish. Dad asked me to hold his line for a second while he went for a beer; taking it, I immediately caught a bright and wiggly porgy, a fish I suspect was already securely hooked when Dad handed me the rod.

As much as he may have enjoyed fishing before I got my hands on him, Dad's enthusiasm was limited by one important fact: he was legally blind. It had happened gradually after the war—why, the doctors couldn't say. Having two young children to support, he had tried to ignore it as long as he could. Driving to work one day, he realized he couldn't see the crossing guards outside an elementary school, and that was it—he never drove a car again. Through a tremendous effort I can only guess at, aided all the way by my mother, he used the blurred remnant of sight that was left to him to continue his career, and succeeded even more importantly at ridding himself of self-pity and despair.

This battle won, his eyesight became the source of some famous mixups, slapstick routines that no one laughed over as much as Dad himself. Most of these occurred at our summer house, and were of such a dramatic and sudden character that they remain etched in our family's memory as a series of tableaux, each with title. There was, for instance, The Time Dad Walked Right Off The End Of The Dock In His Business Suit; The Time Dad Threw Out Mom's Bag Of Jewelry Thinking It Was Garbage; or, most memorably, The Time Dad Snuck Up On His Friend Charlie Beaudrie Floating In An Inner Tube And Dumped Him Over, Only It Wasn't Charlie Beaudrie, It Was A Stranger.

The manmade lake where all this took place was a typical New England resort lake, with summer homes, marinas and camps along one shore, trees, rocks, trout and bass along the other. It was still possible in those years to meet oldtimers who remembered the valley before the lake had been created, but they were dying out fast, and the traditions of that corner of New England were going with them. It was still country in 1963, but the corner had been turned, and in the years we lived there it steadily became more suburban.

Most of our fishing was done at night, after dinner. We'd walk down to the dock together, me weighted down with three rods, a huge tackle box and a lantern; Dad with the landing net and the simple spin-casting rig that was all his eyesight could handle. During the day the lake was blighted with water-skiers and speedboats, but at night it was calm and deserted enough for me to pretend I was in Maine.

"We'll go over to the island," I'd say, nodding sagely (I'd been reading Louise Dickinson Rich's *We Took to the Woods* that summer, and I thought of myself as Gerrish the Guide). "If we don't get lunkers there, we'll head down to the big rock, fish the drop-off. I'll steer. You sit in the back and keep quiet so we don't scare lunkers."

There was no question of Dad's authority in every other aspect of my life, but when it came to fishing, he abdicated all responsibility.

"I think I'll try a popper," Dad would say when we coasted to a stop. He loved catching bluegills.

"No poppers," I'd say, frowning. "We're after bass tonight. We're big-fish fishermen."

Dad would take this all in. "Big-fish fishermen, huh? Okay. Tie on something good."

I had to tie on all Dad's lures, untangle his line, point him in the right direction to cast. I wanted to be patient with him, knew I had to be patient, and yet was never patient enough, and would end up getting more and more irritated with him as the night wore on.

"You're casting too close to shore. Cast further out."

Dad probably couldn't *see* the shore. He'd nod though, and start casting in a different direction.

It would be quiet after that. If the moon were out, our Jitterbugs would glide across the milky beams as gracefully as swans. Occasionally, the wake would reach us from night-cruising boats further out— easy swells that gently rocked us, then draped themselves across the rocks near shore. It was peaceful, but frightening. I had a friend whose father had explained the facts of life to him when fishing one night, and I was afraid that Dad would choose the same time and place for his explanation.

"You're not making your plug gurgle enough," I'd say, hoping to keep the conversation strictly on fishing. "Make it gurgle more."

He'd reel a little faster.

"There's too much moonlight out," I complained. "Fish don't bite in moonlight."

"Last week you said moonlight was good."

"Not above seventy degrees. What's that?"

"What's what?"

"You have a bite! Hook him!"

Dad, who could see neither the plug nor the commotion behind it, would raise his rod tip so gently and timidly that it would infuriate me.

"Sock it to him! Pump him in!"

"What is it?" Dad would say, peering over the side.

"It's gone! Why didn't you reel harder?"

Dad would smile as broadly as if he had caught it. "It was a keeper."

"You lost him," I'd say accusingly. "You lost a bass."

There was no way Dad could win. If he lost the fish, I was furious at him; if he landed it, I was jealous. Luckily for both of us, the fish were few and far between. We'd try every lure in my tackle box, run from one end of the lake to the other, and invariably return empty-handed. It would be ten or eleven by the time we quit. The few simple tasks that Dad could do without help were important to him, so I would wait on the end of the dock while he buttoned the rain-cover over the boat, staring up at the stars—the stars that he couldn't see. We would walk back along the dark road to our house, Dad's shoulder jostling mine as he tripped and caught himself, the lantern swinging circles of light back and forth before our shoes. Holly, our golden retriever, would have the scent of us now and be barking in delight. My mother would be reading by the fireplace, ready with her inevitable question.

"Catch anything?"

"It was a moral victory," I'd say. "Dad had a bite."

And Dad would tell her about it, laughing gently over how excited I had become.

I continued insufferable for the next five summers. Dad would no sooner catch up with my latest theory than I would switch it, insist that night-fishing was for amateurs, demand we go out at dawn, use spinners rather than plugs. I started fly-casting when I was fifteen, and my clumsy efforts imperiled his head, yet he continued fishing from the stern as patiently as before, marveling at my new skill. He even went so far as to buy his own fly rod at Macy's—alone, without my advice. The salesman sold him the wrong kind of line and the wrong kind of reel, and I don't think Dad ever took it out of its case.

By the time I was sixteen I was starting to catch more fish. Plastic worms fished slow were my latest tactic, and for a change I had one that worked. I tried getting Dad to use them, too, but his eyesight wasn't good enough for him to see the line peeling off the spool when a bass took, and he never acquired the knack of sensing a strike with his rod. Still, he took as much pleasure in my fish as if he had caught them himself, and would tell all our friends about my accomplishments, making me nearly burst from pride. His unselfishness was gradually softening my ferocity; I began to need the look of delighted surprise that swept over his face on those rare occasions when he caught a good fish.

In the meantime, Dad's store of misadventures was steadily increasing. There was The Time Dad Hooked An Immense Trout, Only It Wasn't A Trout, It Was A Cris-Craft; The Time Dad, Fishing Without A License, Struck Up A Conversation With The Game Warden; and The Night The Boat Sank.

This last was especially traumatic. We were fishing again at night, and had anchored along the western, uninhabited shore. My Uncle Buzz had come along with us. I had just reeled in the first fish—a catfish, the only one I've ever caught, a mustachioed, portentous creature that we fastened onto a stringer attached to the boat's side.

It was an omen, but we weren't sure of what. We continued casting, listening as usual to one of Uncle Buzz's war stories.

"We had catfish like that in New Guinea. These crackers from Alabama would catch them on doughballs. I remember this other time over in New Caledonia this sergeant, name of Runnels..."

I wasn't listening. There was water sloshing around the bottom of the boat, and I had stood up on the seat to keep my brand-new moccasins dry. Now, though, the water was lapping over my feet again, and I was annoyed. Annoyed, not scared. I took off my moccasins and continued casting.

Ignorance is bliss. The boat had been at the marina earlier in the week being repaired for engine trouble. The mechanic had neglected to replug the drain hole in the stern—a hole we didn't even know existed. Planing at full speed, the hole was above the water line, but the moment we stopped, the boat settled, allowing the water to flow in. A frogman boring a hole in the bottom couldn't have sabotaged us any better.

Buzz was too busy telling war stories to notice anything was wrong. Dad, of course, couldn't see. That left me. The water was up to my shins now, and I was beginning to realize that something important was happening. I had just finished reading Walter Lord's *A Night to Remember* about the *Titanic* disaster, and I was very concerned not to do anything that would cause panic.

"Uh," I said, as casually as I could, "we're sinking."

The water was up to our knees and rising fast. Uncle Buzz hopped into the stern to see what was wrong, which was precisely what he shouldn't have done, since the added weight made us sink faster. I fought my way through the water to the steering wheel, intending to get us closer to shore before we went under. Dad, though, had always had this phobia about ramming our propeller on an underwater rock, and he yelled for me to cut the engine. We were about fifty yards from shore now, and the bow was rising slowly in the air as the stern sank.

Remembering how many people had been pulled under by the *Titanic*'s suction, I climbed onto the side with the intention of jumping clear. I was on the point of leaping . . . I was up to three in my count . . . when the water suddenly came to me, and I felt the side drop away beneath my feet.

Dad and Uncle Buzz had been deposited in the water, too; all we could see of the boat was the descending bow light. When it met the water, its heat sent up a ghostly kind of steam.

"Are you okay?" Dad shouted.

"I'm okay!" I shouted back. "Are you okay?"

The seat cushions had floated loose. I found one for Dad, then swam back to get one for myself.

"Wait for me, guys!" Uncle Buzz, remembering his Boy Scout training, had grabbed the boat's life ring, and was swimming with it toward shore. What Buzz had forgotten, though, was that the ring was still attached by a line to the boat's side. In effect, he was trying to tow the sunk boat with him, huffing and puffing from the strain.

We disentangled him. I saw my tackle box floating in the moonlight, and made a start for it, but I was too worried about Dad's eyesight to leave him. We formed a little convoy and started paddling toward shore. I yelled "Don't panic!" so much that Dad probably thought I *was* panicking, and he kept talking to me in the kind of soothing, reassuring tone he used with babies.

"Here we go now. Everything's perfectly fine. How you doing? We'll just keep swimming now, nice and easy . . . ."

Reaching shore, we argued over what to do next. It was too far to walk home, and there was no trail through the woods. Water and

pickerel grass streamed off our clothes—we were shivering in the cold.
We decided we would have to call for help.

"Let's not panic!" I kept saying.

"Right," Dad said. "We don't want to scare your mother."

We called for help as apologetically as anyone ever called for help.

"Help!" we yelled in unison. "We're all right, but we need some
help!"

Nothing. We tried again.

"We'd like some help over here, please!"

Dad and Buzz soon got tired of shouting. I continued alone, with
stranger and stranger variations.

"S.O.S! Please acknowledge. S.O.S!"

After about an hour of calling, a passing cabin cruiser heard us. We
were back on our dock a few minutes after that. As meek as they were,
our yells had woken up half the community, and there was a small
crowd waiting for us when we arrived. Some of the women had
blankets. One of the teenagers, no doubt having read the same *Titanic*
book I had, offered me a cigarette. I took it—to this day, it's the only
one I've ever smoked. It was great being a survivor.

Though I didn't realize it at the time, The Night The Boat Sank
marked the turning point in our fishing relationship. Besides my
moccasins, I'd lost a beautiful bait-casting outfit, a fly rod and a tackle
box containing roughly a hundred lures. Losing all this chastened my
pride, and I was never quite so dogmatic and pompous about fishing
again. Then, too, it hadn't been me who had stayed calmest during the
sinking, for all my fantasies about being a guide, nor had it been Buzz,
despite his war stories. The true hero had been Dad.

By the time the boat was dredged up and repaired, the summer was
over. The following year I was working, getting to the lake less and
less. Dad would try to go fishing without me, but with little success. I
would tie big loops of monofilament on his lures so he could thread his
line through them rather than the small eyelets, but I think he used to
confine himself to the spinner my mother would tie on before he left; if
it broke, he would quit and go home. The times we did go fishing

together, I was much gentler with him, realizing at last that the talk
and the being there in the twilight were what counted, not the fish we
didn't catch. The last few years before they sold the summer house, he
had his grandaughter to go fishing with. They would cast off the dock
for sunfish, and he would pull the same hold-my-line-while-I-go-over-
here trick with her that he had used with me in those far-off days on
the *BettyWayna*.

Dad doesn't fish much now. I still call him whenever I catch a big
one on the river, and he is as delighted over it as if he had caught it
himself—no, *more* delighted. And this is the lesson he taught me,
taught me slowly and subtly all those summers in the boat when I cast
and pontificated, cast and fumed. Catching fish is a joy, but what is
even better is having someone you love catch one, when the delight is
doubled. This is the true lesson to be taught a fishing son, more
important than any theory regarding fish or fly, and I hope that one
day I may pass it on to a son as patiently and unselfishly as my father
passed it on to me.

Dad came to Vermont for our wedding in July. I took him fishing on
the river. He got his line tangled. I told him where to cast, and got
mad at him when he reeled in too slow. "Catch anything?" my
mother asked when we got back to the lodge. We hadn't. It was the
best fishing trip of the year.

16

October Nineteenth

OOO

I t's hard to know when to give up on something. A hope, a dream, a
friendship, a love. Each of these has a natural life of its own—they
are apt to begin in obscurity and flow in ways unpredictable to man.
Only their endings sometime enter the realm of our control, and in
exchange for this concluding power we are handed a delicate risk. Say
goodbye too soon and you risk missing the fruition, severing the
feeling before its last echoing chord—the bittersweet afterglow—fades
away. Say goodbye too late and emotion that seemed more concentrated and intense than the purest essence can become diluted and stale,
losing the enchantment it once had over us, losing by this transformation its accurate place in our memory.

So it is with rivers. The beginning of a trout season is ritualistic and
well-defined; the middle takes on a natural rhythm that is closely tied
to the river's life, offering the angler participation but not control. It is
the ending of a trout season, the yearly severing of his connection to
the river, that the fly fisherman must choose for himself. Many states
allow fishing until the end of October, but usually the sport is over
well before that, and the moment the fly fisherman quits for the year
depends on factors more instinctual than any fixed date.

I fished too late last year. The leaves were off the trees, the water
was high and discolored, and the trout were as sluggish as carp. Every
quality that attracts me to fishing—the hope of it, the mystery, the

quick swirling life—was gone, replaced by a cold rushing blankness on which nothing could imprint. What was worse, the blankness stayed with me for the next few months with the tenacity of remorse, blocking my earlier memories of the river with this last wintry impression. It had been a good year, a year full of exploration and delight, but there were those stale, cold afternoons tacked on the end. I had been greedy, pushed the river two or three weeks too far. For a writer, a person trained in endings, the mistake was inexcusable.

Fly fishing, after all, is an attempt to make connection with the life of a river. If that life is gone, the attempt becomes absurd. Howard Walden, in his classic *Upstream and Down*, dismisses autumn fishing as "an evocation of ghosts, a second childhood of the trout season, more like a haunting recollection than a living experience. It is a ghoulish disinterring of something better left buried."

It can certainly be that; fish too late, the ghoulies get you. But there is an equal, opposite risk in giving up on a river too soon. A fisherman subscribing to Walden's dictum would have the trout season end with the last small hatch in late summer, thereby cutting himself off from a month and more of fine weather, and trout that still rise willingly to a fly. On my river, quitting too early would mean losing out on some of the year's best days, cloudless, exhilarating afternoons that I would give anything to have back come December. A trout season is an accumulation of puzzles, some of which can still be solved in the fishing's last few days. Quit too early on these and the answers may not be offered again. It doesn't matter if trout are scarce. A fly-fishing season begins in unfulfilled expectation sharpened by optimism; it should end in unfulfilled expectation softened by acceptance.

Vermont's autumn trout season is controversial from a conservation point of view—there are spawning brookies and browns to protect—but there is a fundamental rightness about it in one respect: October is the quintessential Vermont month, and it is a fit and proper feeling to be wading one of its rivers with red leaves at your back. I am not a hunter—my means of assimilating the outdoors is a fly rod, and I want to be able to wield it as far into the autumn as new impressions endure.

"One last time," I said to myself that morning as I got into the car. It was the 19th now, we had had our first hard frosts, and on the summit ridges of the White Mountains east of us I could see faint tracings of snow. Goodbyes were on my mind. I drew out all the rituals of my fishing day as far as they would go—the scrambled eggs and cranberry muffins at the diner, the stop at Sanborn's for new leaders, the drive upstream along the river, the donning of my waders, the careful preparation of line and fly. "One last time," I said, and it transformed even the most banal of my routines into bittersweet farewells.

I began further upstream than I usually go; on this last day I was anxious to have the river where it was comprehensible and small. That it wasn't the fishiest spot on the river didn't bother me. What I wanted was the view of the village across the fields, the white church steeple rising over the elms, the Holsteins grazing by the overgrown stone walls—the milkmaid, the arbor and the meadow.

It was a trout that brought me back to the fishing. I had on a wet fly, the first I had used all year, and a small brook trout had grabbed it as it dangled downstream. I hadn't been concentrating; the sudden tug on the line affected me exactly like a sudden tug on the sleeve—it was as if the trout were mad at me for not doing my part.

I turned my attention back to the river. It was easy to total up all the things that were gone. The leaves, for one. There were great gaps in the foliage, whole trees that were already bare. A New England autumn can be so colorfully full that you forget the curtains of red are supported by a framework of limbs, and their reappearance—stark and straggly—is always something of a shock. The new abundance of light affects you the same way. In summer, the sun on the river comes in shafts, glimmers and reflections; in mid-October, it's everywhere, hidden by no leaves, merged with high white clouds into a sky that seems freshly painted. Had there even been a sky in July? There was no boundary to this October light, and it seemed to well up from the river's bottom just as exuberantly as it poured down from the sun.

There was still a lot of foliage to admire, most of it in the river. I caught my share. On every third or fourth cast, my fly would snare a maple leaf the current was sweeping downstream. Some leaves were real monsters, with pendulous edges and thick fatty stems; others were little fry, miniature leaves that could have fit on a stamp. As I pulled them in, my line tightened and they skittered across the river's surface like miniature kites trying one last time to become airborne.

The insects were gone. The big hatches of spring end by mid-July, but there is a great deal of lesser activity right through the first few frosts. The long decline in their numbers is never final—I have seen insects dancing over the river's surface on warm days in December—but early October seems to mark a turning point in their domination. Until then, there is at least one variety of insect whose predictable appearance makes it worth imitating; after that, the river seems as devoid of bugs as it does fish. Nothing swarms over by the far bank, no clouds hover an inch above the river, and nothing plops from the tree limbs into the eddies to be inhaled instantly.

The autumnal insect in Vermont is the wooly caterpillar—the thick orange and black beastie whose "fur" is supposed to be an infallible guide to the upcoming winter's severity. (It's a superstition I don't take much stock in; their fur is always thick, and predicting a long winter in New England is not exactly going out on a limb.) You see these caterpillars trying to inch their way across the roads this time of year. I've caught lots of October trout on orange and black Wolly Worms fished just below the surface, so at least a few of them must find their way into the river.

And speaking of flies, by October there are great gaps in all my fly boxes, springs and clips that hold nothing, making it seem as if the flies had died off in the cold or migrated with the real insects they copied. I go through an extravagant quantity of flies in the course of a season, and if I didn't limit myself somehow, I'd quickly go broke. Because of that—because I need a reason to use those experimental flies I couldn't resist last spring—I declare a moratorium on all fly buying as of September first. After that date, I use what's in my box, and buy no replacements until the following year. It works fine for a while—I almost always have enough Wulffs and Muddlers to get me through September. By October, though, most of these have been left in trees or trout, and I'm fishing with the chaff. Bushy monstrosities I tied as a kid, snelled wet flies I found at a flea market, saltwater flies from my days on the Cape—they're all trotted out now, and occasionally a trout will take one from sheer astonishment.

Halfway through the morning I snapped off the wet fly on which I'd caught the brookie. For lack of anything better, I switched to a Daniel Webster. It's a "salter" fly—a green and red bucktail designed for sea-run browns—so I wasn't surprised that I didn't catch anything with it. I contemplated my alternatives. There was a Honey Blonde in a size suited for tarpon; some battered Light Hendricksons, and half a dozen other creations the names of which I had forgotten.

There was one more possibility. In the course of a season's shufflings and unpackings, flies drop out of their boxes and get caught all over the car—in the mat of the trunk, the floor carpets and upholstery. I decided to go back and see what I could glean.

I had waded downstream at a pretty good clip, and it was a long walk to the car. By the time I got there, a hot cup of something was sounding pretty good. I pulled my waders off and got behind the wheel, debating which way to head. A mile east was a general store, but it was a filthy, depressing place. I decided to take a chance and head upriver.

I didn't go very far. About a mile up the road and hanging over it was a banner riddled with holes: OLD HOME DAYS OCT. 18–19. Beyond it was a green arrow pointing to the left; on an impulse, I joined a line of pick-ups and jeeps heading in that direction.

An old farmer with a cane pointed me to a parking spot on a straw-covered field. He was very businesslike. When I tried to take a spot nearer the front, he poked his cane at the car like it was a recalcitrant cow, forcing me back.

The fairground was simply a four-acre field, half of which had been turned into a rough soccer field for the elementary-school team. It was set on a small plateau above the trees, and the temperature in the wind must have been five degrees colder than it had been back in the valley.

It wasn't hard to find the coffee. Boy Scout Troop 82, the "Cobra" troop, was selling it by the abandoned "Dunk A Dummy" booth, and that's where most of the fairgoers were huddled. Warmed, a few of them broke away to watch the soccer game; the local team was being trounced by a bigger squad, but the cheers were good-natured for both sides. Vermont schools often lack the boys to make up an eleven-man team, so girls play, too, and the ones I saw were doing just fine—there was a small, shifty redhead who had a murderous shot from right wing.

The rest of the fair was just getting started. An auctioneer who could have been Robert Frost's brother was unloading junk for the charity auction—some old skis, broken televisions, sleds and shovels. Further up the hill was the tag sale, the vendors sitting on lawn chairs before their merchandise, wrapped in blankets. Behind them was the horseshoe pitching. Though it was still early, a dozen or so games were already in progress, and the clank of shoe hitting stake was the metronomic sound that underlay everything—the distant cheers, the tape-recorded music, the wind.

I found some shelter in a dugout along the first-base side of a diamond that Abner Doubleday might have played on; there was an old-fashioned dirt cutout between the pitcher's mound and home plate, and rickety stands straight out of an 1880s mezzotint. It was a good vantage point. There in right field a crew was setting up the carnival rides and food concessions, testing the neon. Try a Jaffle! one sign urged. None of the fairgoers seemed interested. They were selling ices, taffy and soda; the rides were summertime rides, too, and it all seemed out of place in the wind.

For the carnival, this stop was the end of the line. The larger towns booked for summer, then the medium-sized ones, then the small ones, and then finally—on the last open date before winter—the hill villages like this one, 500 or fewer souls trying to pretend it was still summer.

But it didn't matter, of course. It was all good-natured, the take was for charity, and everyone seemed to be having a good time. Two members of the 4-H club found me in the dugout and sold me a raffle ticket. The word was out after that, and I had to turn down chances offered by the quilt club, the snowmobile club and the Masons. A reporter from the local paper came up to me next. Yes, I was having a good time, I said into his tape recorder. Yes, I thought things were done just fine.

We talked for a while after that. He was upset about his assignment—he would have much preferred to be down at Dartmouth for the football game. Still, it was kind of nice with the kids and the leaves and all. His daughter was a Rainbow Girl and if I wanted to buy a chance on a new wood stove, he'd send her over.

I stayed long enough for another cup of Boy Scout coffee, then started back to the river. I was still ambivalent about fishing. The morning hadn't been very productive, and I was worried about pushing the river too hard again, prolonging the season past the point of reasonable expectation and reward.

But I couldn't quit, not yet. When I was a boy, we would drive back to the city from our weekend home on Sunday afternoons; in following the lake, I would see men going out in boats to fish, fly rods sticking out from the stern, their parkas puckered tight around their chins. I would envy them, wanting nothing so much as to be out there, too, in the October wind. To be able to do what appeared to me the very epitome of freedom, and autumn afternoons have generated the same yearning ever since.

"One more time," I said, for the second time that day. I went into the river three miles upstream of the stretch I had fished in the morning. I was getting up into the headwaters now—the water was six or seven feet wide at the most. The falls, rapids and pools were all miniaturized, and I fished downstream expecting nothing bigger than miniature trout.

I had on a tattered white nymph I had found in my box under some Irresistibles. In this kind of water, tactics aren't complicated—do what's necessary to keep the fly in place, and the rest is up to the trout. Thus, I concentrated on letting the nymph dangle worm-like in the deep spots, and did my best to avoid the leaves.

There was nothing for the first hundred yards. The pools deepened slightly as I moved downstream, until I came to the deepest of the stretch: a slow, hemlock-shaded glide between matching boulders. I fished the far side of the left boulder without a rise. I fished the far side of the right boulder—nothing there, either. There remained one possibility. Letting line out slowly, I swam the nymph in the dark channel between boulders, and—so perfect was the spot—hooked the fish in my imagination a moment before the real trout took hold.

One of the delights of hooking a fish on a nymph is that for the first few seconds you gain no impression of its size. The current had tightened the line enough to set the hook, but the trout's first movement was upstream toward me, and I had to reel in fast in order to get to the point where I could feel him. It was this moment—the instant when the line came taut and I sensed his weight and power, sensed, that is, a life beyond my expectation—that was the best of the fight.

The rest was interesting enough. A trout that size in such narrow water could easily have broken free, at least in a big-river style of fight. But by some accommodation I couldn't penetrate, the fish geared his struggle to the miniaturized stream, and confined his runs to short, flashing darts between rocks. As usual, I was fishing a 6X leader—the merest gossamer—so I didn't dare force him. I waded from rock to rock, flushing him with my wader boot, gaining eight or nine inches of line before he made it to the next rock in our progression.

Space was on my side. The water was getting shallower as the river widened, and each rock gave the trout less protection. After ten more minutes of tag, I urged him gently toward shore, and he was tired enough to go along. The rocks gave way to wet stones that eased his transition from water to land; I nudged him onto the sand, and he lay there gasping in the mingled surprise and fear with which the first prehistoric fish must have flopped from the sea.

A rainbow and a good one—fifteen inches, with a thick, streamlined flank and a brightness fresh as the sky. For that part of the river, a very big fish indeed.

I looked around for a rock large enough to kill him. It's a tradition with me; I release all but three or four of the trout I catch each year, but the last one is to be taken home, cleaned, cooked and eaten, thereby reminding me of exactly where in the food chain I stand. (I have an anthropologist friend who refers to my fishing as "hunting and gathering," and at some basic, instinctual level she is right.) I had the rock in my hand—I had picked out the spot on his head where I would hit him—when for a reason that wasn't immediately evident, I changed my mind.

I took the trout with both hands and brought him back to the water. Kneeling, I swam him into the current, moving his tail back and forth until he had revived sufficiently to hold his place in my loosely cupped hands. We retraced the path of our fight in stages; I held him behind each rock in turn, letting him adjust to the increased pressures before moving him on. It was ten minutes before he was strong enough to release. I started him off with an encouraging shove, and this time there was no flank-turning, sideways retreat back to my hands—he swam off powerfully toward the depths of the pool.

It wasn't until I saw him swim away that I found my reason for releasing him. Winter was coming, and I wanted to be able to sit at my desk and picture him there in his dark pool, enduring the snow and ice as patiently as I did, waiting for spring with the same kind of certainty and hope, my emissary to May.

Winter. It was in the river now—the light was washed from it, the warmth and life. I had my reel off and my rod unjointed before I reached the bank.

A good season. It was time to get out.

17

A Tracer of Streams

∞

One could do worse than be a tracer of streams. Following a river to its source through every winding, battling flood, drought and disease, a Livingston in moral fervor, a Burton in intelligence, opening up to human imagination a country spacious enough for a million dreams, pinning down its origins on a map heretofore blank, sharing the journey in a book more adventurous than any *Odyssey*— they have always been epic tasks, fit for the Lewises and Clarks of the world, the Stanleys and the Spekes.

To those who only know it in its navigable reaches, a great river's source is among the most unimaginable of things, an Ultima Thule we can never picture, so small and obscure is that first irreversible impulse that gives it life. The Hudson is the river that flows past the skyscrapers of Manhattan a thousand yards wide, but it is also that portion of the small waterfall high in the Adirondacks which, splashing on a convex rock, follows the right-hand grooves south.

To follow great rivers to their source was my boyhood dream. I pictured myself a mountain climber dipping my hands in the Andes brook that was the Amazon, letting the water flow off my face before continuing its run down to the sweltering jungle, coming home through great peril to write the book of my adventures. As dreams go, it wasn't a bad one; as time went on, it was less abandoned than transformed. At fourteen, I made the acquaintance of the great writers,

men like Tolstoy and Conrad, and realized that they were following streams to their source as well—streams of character, history and fate, on journeys every bit as difficult as the greatest explorer's. It was this kind of trip I eventually embarked on, starting off into the jungle with a rusty machete, a wobbly compass, rebellious bearers and no guides, but with all the hope in the world.

And yet there turned out to be a river in it after all—the river of this book. It is no Missouri or Nile, not even a Hudson, but a gentle trout river flowing from modest mountains in the small state where I live. I went to it first partly as a relief from the expeditionary labor of writing—the tracing of various threads through novels and stories— but in time, the river began to seem a thread worth writing about on its own, linking as it did not only the separate, sunlit afternoons when I fished it, but the memories of fishing that lay scattered across my life without locus. In writing about the river through the seasons, I had been trying to trace it to its source just as surely as if I were hiking along its banks, map in hand. The river at dusk, the river in August, the river in fall—these were all windings that had to be explored if I was to reach the elusive spring that was its beauty's source.

At the same time I was following the river in a figurative sense, I was following it in a literal one. The fishing season's impulse was upstream—each afternoon seemed a bit above the one that preceded it, until by October I was fishing the river where it was only a few yards wide. Below me the river was familiar through a hundred trips, but upstream the water was always new, and I waded through it with increasing delight.

I had made the resolution to hike to the river's source as I stood by its banks in a February snowstorm, but the time had never seemed propitious. Spring meant black flies, mosquitoes and mud; summer brought heat, and September had been crowded with too much fishing. Beyond these reasons was my own insistence on doing things in the right order. I wanted to find the spring or pond that was the river's source only when the rest of it was thoroughly explored, saving that final expedition as the cap on all my experiences. The moment would come when striking out for the headwaters would seem as natural and unpremeditated as fishing a slightly higher pool, and I trusted my instincts enough to wait.

I went the same October afternoon I released the big rainbow. It was on an impulse—it wasn't until I was in the car driving west that I understood what had prompted me. As curious as I was to find the source, I had been waiting until the fishing was over for the year so I could walk the river's banks without feeling compelled to wonder about its trout. In fly fishing, each pool and rapid becomes momentarily the entire world, curiosity is localized, and the rest of the river may as well not exist—we fish in fragments of space just as we do fragments of time. Fishing was the medium that had taught me most about the river, but now, in trying to grasp a larger section, it would only be in the way.

The road stayed by the river at first. There's a small hill town where the valley starts to narrow. I had thought of it as having the neat, rectangular perfection of a village on a model train layout, but that was in summer, and without the camouflage of leaves, the homes looked battered and exposed. Beyond its outskirts, I came to the summit of the river's main valley. At the top, the road joins another road that crosses it like a T, changing the trend from vaguely east-west to vaguely north-south. The river's channel was less obvious than before, but I knew from studying the map that it was still somewhere off to my right. A few miles after turning, I crossed it on a highway bridge. It wasn't parallel to the road anymore, but at a right angle to it, racing down through a dark tunnel of spruce. I was tempted to park my car there and follow it through the woods, but then decided to see if I could pick it up again further upstream.

It was a different country I was driving through, an open, lonely tableland that had more of Montana in it than Vermont. For some unknown reason, I had expected the river to become more like itself as it neared the top, and the transformation from pastoral, meadowed valley to rugged, timbered plateau took me by surprise. Signs of man were few. There was a fallen-down, roofless barn with the words "Barn Dance!" scrawled across it in mocking red paint; a cemetery whose headstones just barely cleared the weeds; a bullet-scarred road sign announcing a change in counties. Other than that, nothing—just two quiet mountains with cloud shadows laying across their synclines like heavy wool blankets.

The river started somewhere high in the folds of those slopes. I drove the highway to the top of the height of land, looking for a road or trail that would branch off in the right direction. I went too far—over the summit of the plateau, down into the beginnings of a separate watershed. Turning around, I came upon a dirt road that looked promisingly obscure. It was worth a try—in Vermont, dirt roads head toward water with the sure instinct of thirsty cattle let loose on a Texas plain. There were too many ruts and washouts to drive it. Leaving the car on the edge of the pavement, I got out and started to walk.

I went about a mile before I picked up the river. The road ran toward the mountains' base through a meadow-like expanse of second-growth timber, spikey larch on the verge of turning amber, and gnarled apple trees that had survived every cutting. Every now and then I would see a bullet casing in the leaves by the edge of the road, gleaming like golden chips dropped by hunters so they could retrace their way. But for once there were no bottle or beer cans to go with them, no roaring power saws, no harsh reminders of the land's misuse.

There was a stream where the road first dipped, but it was too small to be the river proper, so I kept walking. About ten minutes later, I came to the main stream, or at least its bed. It was five feet wide here, nearly empty. It hadn't rained in several weeks, and there was even less water in the center of the rocks than there was in the tributary. Still, it was obviously my river—I walked upstream just far enough to make sure its course aimed for the sag in the mountains where the map said it began. There wasn't time to follow it now. It had been a successful reconnaissance, and in the morning I would be back.

Or so I thought. At dawn, the drumming of rain on the roof made the thought of bushwacking through the woods less appealing than it had seemed the night before; my exploratory impulse firmly under control, I turned over and went back to sleep. The rain continued for three days, then business interfered, so it wasn't until the end of the month that I was able to get back: Halloween, as it turned out—a fit day for mad enterprises of every kind.

I parked at the same place I had on my first trip, and hiked the dirt road to the river beneath the first blue sky in days. The rain had changed the equation. Instead of a dehydrated trickle, I found a racing mountain torrent that in places was over its banks. This was both good and bad. Good in that it seemed more recognizably my river; bad because I no longer had a dry staircase of rocks to climb to the top. I went through my pack to make sure I had a compass, tied my climbing shoes tighter for good luck, then—taking a deep breath—started off into the woods.

It was easy going at first. There was a deer trail parallel to the banks, and little of the underbrush I had been afraid would slow me down. The river was only a few feet wide here, but the pools were deep, and the rapids strong enough to cover the obvious fords. I hiked an hour before the volume of water appreciably slackened; after that, I could count on finding a place to cross every few yards.

Without leaves to block it, the sun was surprisingly warm, and it wasn't long before I peeled off my sweater. Like most Vermont hillsides, this one had once been farmed—there was the inevitable stone wall buried in forest detritus, the telltale apple trees lost amid maple, the barely discernible cellar holes choked with vines. With the leaves gone, the birch stood out with more flair than they had earlier in the fall; their white was more frequent the higher you looked, making it seem as if they were marching in formation up the slopes. It's an effect I enjoy. For all the talk of foliage, Vermont only seems itself—its gritty, unadorned, spare self—when October's extended shrug is over and the leaves are finally renounced.

It was only during breaks that I was able to give the scenery the attention it deserved. The rest of the time I walked with my eyes down, concentrating on the terrain one or two steps ahead. Most of the hiking I had done lately was in the White Mountain trails over in New Hampshire, and it was much easier; the trails were well-marked and graded, and—at least on the easier ones—you could stroll along without worrying what your feet were up to. Here, every step had to be selected with care. Flat boulders turned out to wobble when stepped on; firm-looking logs had a trick of disintegrating. Twist an ankle in the Whites and another hiker would eventually come along and help you; twist an ankle on these rocks, and it would mean a very cold, lonely night to contemplate my mistake. I was going slow to start with, and after getting a foot wet when a boulder used as a bridge unexpectedly rolled sideways, I went even slower. I began to worry that I might not have time to reach the source after all.

I had crossed the river thirteen times, and was preparing to cross it a fourteenth when I realized that the bank I was following flattened out up ahead into a clearing. This was a change in the established pattern. Always before, the bank would remain level for several hundred yards, then dramatically steepen as the river began to curve, forcing me to cross over to the other bank in order to make any progress. I was zigzagging, walking more sideways than uphill.

This time, I decided to continue on until I came to the clearing. A deer yard, I assumed, but no—rather than closing in a circle, it shaped itself into a funnel pointing upstream. It was an old logging road, one of those providential passageways you often come on in New England just when the bushwhacking turns ridiculous. It was unquestionably the oldest, bushiest, most obscure logging road I had ever encountered, but I was thankful for it just the same—it speeded up my pace by several m.p.h. It took the path of least resistance up the valley, sometimes hugging the river, sometimes crossing it, sometimes running away from it up the ridge. Times it ran away, I stuck to the river; after following it so long, it had become like one of those nature walks for the blind you see in the national parks, a rope guiding me through the forest which I dared not let go. Sticking to the river meant scrambling over granite ledges, climbing blowdowns and hopping rocks, but it was worth it—more than anything, I needed to stay in touch with that bright, racing ribbon to which I felt increasingly tied. A hundred yards of hard going and the logging trail would rejoin the stream, easing my way.

I crossed the river three more times before taking a break. Each ford was a new challenge; picking a way across the river required the same kind of half-premeditated, half-instinctual route-finding climbers use in scaling a cliff, and the same kind of balance. The trick was in finding a bridge of stones that led slightly upstream, so that you were crossing from lower rocks onto higher ones, thereby keeping your inertia within reasonable bounds. Hop downstream and the tendency was to keep going head-over-heels; hop upstream and gravity acted like a pair of cushioning arms. The best kinds of fords were where the rocks were flat, but far enough apart so you didn't take them for granted; the trickiest were the ones where the banks were closest together, tempting you into a jump. At the less obvious fords, I tried making bridges out of whatever log was handy, but this was time-consuming, and by continuing upstream I could usually find a place where the crossing was easier.

The scale of the river was changing the further up it I hiked. I no longer made diminishing comparisons to the broad stretches where I fished, but began taking it on its own; if anything, its sound and light filled that narrow valley more completely than it did further downstream. The lower water shared the landscape with farms, highways and towns, but here near the source the river was everything—the dominant fact—and it seemed to paradoxically widen in my imagination the narrower it became, until finally there was nothing else in my senses but that bouncing, impetuous flow.

I stopped for lunch on a small island around which the river divided itself in mossy, inch-deep riffles. A family of grouse had beaten me to the driest patch of leaves; hearing me, they burst away in five scattered directions. I opened my pack and took out an apple and some cheese. There was a log behind me that doubled as backrest and table. Thirsty, I drank right from the stream, cupping my hands under the tiny falls until the water bubbled off my wrists. The water had the flavor of transparency. Swallowing it, I wasn't aware of taste, but only idea: purity. Purity had a cool feel on the lips, and nourished a delicious sense of well-being. Purity ran down my skin and made me shiver. Purity made me drink again and again, as if from a well I wanted to prove was endless.

Sitting there, I had a chance to watch the river more carefully. The rain of the previous week had washed down thousands of small twigs, and the water was still deciding where to put them. Some of the thicker ones were already jammed into a miniature dam; as I watched, smaller twigs were swept into it and gently tucked by the current underneath the upstream edge, weaving the dam even thicker. With the river at its smallest, even a foot-long branch was a major impediment, and the banks were grooved with dry, alternate channels the water had explored and abandoned in its drive downhill.

My thoughts were following it now, gradually widening my focus from the small, hemlock-shaded island where I sat in the same way the river's banks gradually widened, admitting more and more. It was an aerial view I was aiming toward—a perspective from somewhere up above those trees. The river was a mountain brook running through a forest abandoned when the white men who settled it in the 1780s moved west a century later. The river was an upland stream moving past the hill towns of two hundred people that still clung to life in a remote valley of rural Vermont. The river was a medium-sized trout stream running through the Green Mountain foothills to a junction with the Connecticut. The river was one of hundreds flowing down the ocean side of the ancient Appalachian chain on the east coast of the United States. The river was one of thousands lining the continent, one of millions creasing the earth—a microscopic gram of hydrogen and oxygen lost in an immensity of waterless stars. A grain of water in the universe, a thread of water on the planet, a small river in North America, a trout stream in the Appalachians, a mountain brook in Vermont, and that brought it all the way back down to me, sitting there against the damp husk of a long-dead oak, wondering where the hell in this immense scheme I fit.

And what about me? What was this insignificant scruffy atom of consciousness thinking about as it telescoped so glibly up to the stars and so precipitously back down again? I was thinking about the opening day of the trout season back in April—how conscious I had been of my boyhood dream of being able to fish a trout stream at will and the dream's fruition, the actual river itself, icy, powerful and real. In between were long years in the city when the only rivers I knew were vicarious ones, just vivid enough to keep the dream alive and torment me by their ever more doubtful realization. The visits I made to real rivers only reminded me of what I was missing, and by my mid-twenties, I was beginning to talk about trout fishing as something I *used* to do. A lover of streams, a good caster, a fan of trout, a reader of all the right books and where was I? Stuck in the city, bitterly wishing.

But the thing about dreams is that you never know. Herman Melville, an old man living forgotten in New York, had above his study desk the motto "Be true to the dreams of thy youth." I had another boyhood dream besides fishing: I wanted to write. Pursuing it took all my energy and courage for ten hard years. Slowly, taking three steps back for every advance, I managed to establish a career. With it came freedom; I was able to move to the country, and there in the hills above my home found the river, the second of my boyhood dreams, trailing along in this first dream's fulfillment. The beautiful mountains, a woman I loved . . . It was as if the dream of writing had been dreamt so intensely that it had established a force-field powerful enough to tug other dreams in its wake, a balm for the bitterness the yearning engendered.

And so I was thinking how lucky I was to be sitting there contemplating the overlapping valleys, metaphorical and real, the river connected. The other thing about dreams is their shortness, but that was all right, too. I had my dream as few people ever had theirs, and though it should only last this one season, I was going to get it down on paper once and for all.

The wind was coming up now—I felt it on the back of my neck as the gentle pressure from a woman's hand. It was time to start hiking again. But there was one more thing I wanted to work through before leaving. It concerned a trout, a fourteen-inch brown trout that appears nowhere else in this book. I caught him on a Cinammon Ant in the late afternoon of a late August day, and had been trying to put him out of my mind ever since. In playing him, I was never so aware of a trout's being—its strength and beauty, its single-minded impulse toward life, its perfect coexistence with water. I was torn between wanting him to break loose and wanting to have him in my hand before letting him go. As it turned out, he was gut-hooked, already bleeding from the gills by the time I beached him. I took a rock from the bank and quickly finished the job.

Happy and sad, happy and sad, the inevitable conjunction! I had felt the life of that trout so intensely because he was dying; the strange sympathy that links hunter and hunted had been in full force for those few moments we were connected, and I felt severed when his life dropped away. Even something as harmless as fishing comes down to it in the end: the bitter and the sweet, the pleasant memory tinged with sadness, the trout living and the trout dead.

With luck, I would know and love the river for many years to come. Never would I live it with the same intensity. My dream had reached its apogee with the hooking of that trout, and by the time I took the rock and killed him, another bit of boy in me was gone.

I shouldered my rucksack and started up the eastern bank. The sun had gotten around behind me while I was resting, and its lower edge was disappearing below the trees on the ridge. I walked faster now, taking fewer detours as the logging trail stayed closer to the stream. The climbing was less strenuous than before. After that first narrow valley, the terrain had flattened out into a gently sloping plateau. A steep climb around waterfalls would have indicated the source was near; this easier grade meant the river was less hurried, its energy conserved, its source further off than I had thought.

Eventually, the logging trail trickled out, and I began bushwhacking through vines, brush and trees, forcing my way rather than finding it. I resented even the slightest detour now—the river seemed the one life in the forest besides mine, and I hated to let it go. The stream bed was shallower, not as rocky and well-defined as it had been lower down; it wasn't cutting through the hillside as much as racing over it, and judging by the ferns and moss growing well to either side of its present course, it often slid a bit to the right or left, depending on its mood.

With the fading daylight, the increasing cold, my journey up the river was taking on the quality of a race. I tried to slow myself down, took frequent breathers, but there was nothing I could do about the adrenalin I felt pumping through me each time I stopped. As it had so many times before, the river itself forced me to adopt an easier pace. Two hours after I stopped for lunch, I came upon the first significant falls. They weren't high—four feet at the most—but in the reduced scale I was traveling through, they loomed as large as Niagara must have to those early voyageurs trying to work their way up the Great Lakes.

Above the falls was a surprise: three channels, each as full of water as the one I had been following. I felt like Lewis and Clark at the headwaters of the Missouri: disappointed that the main river didn't continue; curious as to which of the tributaries led furthest west.

There was nothing for it but to explore each in turn. The left fork—the one that ran perpendicularly west from the falls—looked promising, but soon petered out into a leaf-choked channel of mud. Retracing my way downstream, I started up the middle fork, the one that ran straightest into the falls. This time I hiked a strenuous half-mile before the water ran out. It was a pretty little brook, probably nonexistent when it didn't rain, and obviously not the main branch.

So it was the right-hand fork after all. The minute I started along it, I knew it was my river—there was a life and impetus to it the other two branches didn't have. And since I had been forced to explore each of them, the time lost was vital. It was obvious now that I wasn't going to reach the source, not today. The river was dwindling, but in an unhurried way, and the underbrush along both banks was getting harder to penetrate the higher I climbed. Even if I turned back now, it would be dark by the time I got below the island, and I would have to grope the rest of the way back to my car.

Still, it was hard to stop. The further up the river I traveled, the more private and secret it seemed. I felt I was approaching an answer that had long eluded me, at the stage where the solution was almost in sight, requiring no further decisions or agonized puzzling out, but only endurance... that it was there and there was nothing left to reaching it but sheer endurance. I would stop, turn my back on it, start downhill, then turn around and start climbing again, resolved to go just a little bit further.

The fourth stop was my last. There are mountain summits in the Himalayas that are sacred to the peoples living at their base; climbers, respecting this, stop a foot short of the summit, leaving that final temple of snow forever virgin. It was out of this same worshipful impulse that I turned back from the source. I would never know the river so well that I would lose my awe of its beauty, and it was right that its last few yards—its inviolable beginning—remained a mystery to me still.

I straddled the river, a leg on each side, then slowly bent down to dip my hands ceremoniously in the water, letting the pure, cold drops roll down my fingers back into the flow from which they came.

A few things more, the light growing fainter. A leaf brushing my neck on its way to the ground . . . a woodpecker rattling a tree in the distance behind me . . . the wind in the pines as it came down off the mountain . . . the sound of the river . . . a last quiet look . . . and all the rest is simply going home.